Drama Acr

Drama Across the Curriculum

Anita Goerecke

Illustrated by Daniel Cardone

Longman Cheshire

Longman Cheshire Pty Limited
Longman House
Kings Gardens
95 Coventry Street
Melbourne 3205 Australia

Offices in Sydney, Brisbane, Adelaide and Perth. Associated
companies, branches and representatives throughout the world.

Designed by Tony Palmer
Set in 11 pt Frutiger 55
Produced by Longman Cheshire Pty Ltd
Printed in Malaysia — GPS

National Library of Australia
Cataloguing-in-Publication data

Goerecke, Anita.
  Drama across the curriculum.

  Bibliography.
  ISBN 0 582 90983 X.

  1. Drama—Study and teaching (Primary). I. Title.

372.66043

These symbols represent a broad guide to the age groups for which
activities in this book are most suitable. Activities should be adapted
and extended to suit different ability levels.

○ about 5–7 year olds

□ about 7–9 year olds

△ about 10–12 year olds

To Daniel and Simon and all the other children in my life
for their inspiration

Contents

Preface

Primary teachers are teachers of Drama. In my years of classroom teaching there has rarely been a time when Drama has not been happening in my room or in classrooms around me. Colleagues who say they do not 'do' Drama have unknowingly used the process in their teaching for years in all areas of the curriculum. The moment teachers use words like 'imagine' or 'pretend', or say, 'What would happen if. . .', they venture a little way into the dramatic process. It is an enabling process which capitalises on children's natural curiosity and ability to imagine and leads them from what they know to the challenge of the unknown and to new understandings.

Drama Across the Curriculum is not about how to teach Drama; it is about how to explore concepts in Environment, Society, Science and Mathematics imaginatively and creatively. English Language is not a separate unit in the book since the development of language skills is intrinsic to the Drama process and already incorporated within each unit. In fact, every unit is a language unit as well as a Science or Maths unit. The book is an activity approach which demonstrates ways to make abstract concepts/issues more tangible for children by using Drama to introduce, reinforce or evaluate understandings.

The activities encourage co-operation between children and teacher, their knowledge, personality and language guiding the lesson to a conclusion appropriate to class needs. The activities are not meant to be prescriptive. In fact, the outcome may not necessarily be that described in an activity—the questioning lends itself to a wide range of possibilities. The important thing is that it works within the children's sphere of experience and the teacher's teaching situation.

Using drama methodology to teach concepts across the primary school curriculum has worked for me. I invite you and your class to explore and experiment with the ideas in *Drama Across the Curriculum* and use the activity format as a guide to creating your own Drama.

1
Introduction

Format of the activities

The activities in *Drama Across the Curriculum* are meant to be flexible so teachers can use them to suit their own needs. The open-ended nature of tasks and the issues covered can be dealt with in different ways by children according to their age and ability. Age level codes which precede each activity are therefore a broad guide and activities should be adapted and extended in keeping with children's abilities.

Each activity is complete in itself and any one can be used as a starting point. In some units there are two or three sequenced activities identified by (a), (b) or (c). These have a follow-through theme and can be taught in sequence or alone.

The numbered points within each activity are designed according to logical progression based on the questioning. However, since children's responses differ in each situation this may be used as a guide to assist with the progression of the lesson towards development of a particular concept.

The **Teacher talk** sections are only examples of language which can be used to set up a lesson or to further concept development. The teacher's own language and expression is vitally important and intrinsic to the Drama process. However, the talk should be kept brief as it is in the book and be used only to facilitate children's involvement in the doing of Drama.

Resources

Each activity is accompanied by a list of resources required for its completion. These are not prescriptive but give an indication of the kinds of things that can be used. For the majority of the activities resource materials are kept to a basic minimum in the interest of economy of finances and time. Resources may be added to suit individual needs.

Skills and concepts

Skill development is identified at the beginning of each activity. The skills listed are generally attributed to the curriculum area in which the activities are focused. The list is not exhaustive and children will probably use additional skills as they involve themselves in the activity process. Concepts that are evident in the unit or that may occur as a result of the activity are also listed. The level of development of these concepts is highly dependent on how teacher and children engage in the activity. Concepts may need further consolidation through other activities.

Drama processes

Drama skills and processes occur in all the activities and complement the acquisition of skills in other curriculum areas. Drama processes help children to develop a variety of social and information-seeking skills, for example:

Drama processes	Skills
	problem-solving
Suspension of disbelief	decision-making
	group dynamics
	co-operation
Role	risk-taking
	development of responsibility
	empathy with others
Mime and figuration	hypothesising
	investigating
	researching
Building environments	generalising
	questioning
	organising
Story-making	interacting
	communicating
	planning
Play-building	evaluating
	tolerance
	appreciation
Improvisation	responding/feedback

Examples of how the drama processes are used in the book are on the following page.

Evaluation

There are many methods of assessment but whatever the processes it is essential that evaluation be purposeful, and that who or what is being assessed, and why, be clearly defined. A comprehensive evaluation of a lesson should determine:

(a) the appropriateness and effectiveness of the content and resources;

(b) the children's responses, behaviour and the skills used;

(c) the effectiveness of the processes and skills used by the teacher.

The activities in the units are continually evaluating children on concept/skill acquisition. Questioning is an essential component of every activity in this book and therefore facilitates the use of questioning as a evaluative tool with the natural progression of the lesson. Questioning appraises what is actually happening in the lesson, maximises

Drama Processes

Role
- taking on various known roles, for example mother/father, teacher, etc.
- playing out family/school situations
- taking roles to suit stories, for example an explorer in the jungle.

Building environments
- building a structure to work in using available equipment such as chairs, tables, mats, drama blocks, etc., for example making a jungle/forest/planet to explore

Play-building
- building a story scene by scene, for example
  (a) a family of rabbits at home in a national park
  (b) a land developer organising his tractors
  (c) a group of residents
  How do all of these come together in the same story?

Suspension of disbelief
- going on imaginary journeys and meeting characters in role, for example going on an exploratory journey to a planet and meeting the leader of the planet – the leader could be another adult dressed as the character. (The character's presence is organised by the teacher prior to the beginning of the activity, unbeknown to the children)

Improvisation
- acting out a certain situation
- acting out own personal experience
- story-beginnings: work with a partner/group to make an ending

Story-making
- making up a story to suit a particular topic/concept and acting it out
- making up stories to suit an environment or character

Mime and figuration
- becoming inanimate objects and being used by others in stories, for example becoming household appliances and being used by people
- acting out stories without words, for example doing occupational mimes such as workers/shoppers, etc.
- miming daily activities

learning experiences and helps to realise objectives. Evaluation should be continuous and ongoing to be truly effective and not only occur at the end of the lesson.

Before beginning the activities it is important to be aware of the factors in a lesson requiring evaluation which subsequently guide evaluative questioning. The questions in *Drama Across the Curriculum* are likely to produce a variety of responses which demonstrate understandings beyond the specific curriculum concepts and are reflective of the Drama focus. Responses could include information about children's verbal and non-verbal communication skills, physical, emotional and intellectual abilities and understandings, and also highlight their ability to interact socially, project themselves into imaginary roles and situations, and to solve problems creatively. It is the evaluation of these factors which guides and determines the success of the lesson and provides necessary feedback for future planning. Therefore, how children respond to a question or a task/situation can also determine their level of understanding and their skill development.

Examples of evaluation
A
'In groups of three, children mime the melting rate of a small ice cube in one of the following situations':
  (a) inside the refrigerator (not the freezer compartment)
  (b) on the window-sill on a sunny day
  (c) in a frypan on a hot stove
Observing children in this activity can determine their understanding of the effects of heat but it can also indicate their skills and understandings of the Drama process. For instance, what is their level of absorption in the activity? Can they sustain the Drama? How do the children use language? What do their movements tell you about their confidence and expressive skills, their physical co-ordination or their understanding of Mime?
(For **Example B** see table on page xi.)

C
Checklists and anecdotal records are valuable ways of assessing observable outcomes. However, assessment of the visible signs of effort that each child demonstrates through the dramatic process is only a small indication of the child's achievements since it is impossible to determine all the emotional effort a child makes in a drama experience. This is where a child's self-reporting is extremely valuable, whether it be in written or oral form.

In *Drama Across the Curriculum* the lists of skills and concepts at the beginning of each activity can be used as a

B

Focusing questions	Evaluative questions				
Breathing and living unit	Curriculum concept	Social/emotional	Communication—verbal/non-verbal	Physical	Problem solving
(Explore the sea.) What did you see in the sea environment? What would you do if your air tank stopped working?	Responses reveal the child's knowledge of the sea.	Did the child/children interact co-operatively? Did the child sustain the role? How involved was the child in the role (absorption/concentration)? Did the child show empathy, rapport with others?	Was the child able to communicate using body language? Did the child speak clearly/confidently? Was the child an active listener? Did the child demonstrate different language registers/modes (critical, creative, descriptive, etc.)? Was the language appropriate to the situation?	Is the child co-ordinated? Did the child's movements convey imaginative projection? Does the child move freely (uninhibited)? What degree of control does the child have over body movements (flow, sustain, hold, etc.)?	Were the child's solutions creative/valid? Did the child offer ideas/suggestions? Was the child involved in solving the problem (commitment)?

guide to formulate checklists to show development in particular curriculum areas. The teacher should decide what skill or concept mastery is being assessed and also give consideration to the level of effort individuals produce. In anecdotal records particular mention should be made of what a child can do, knows and understands. Drama skills, however, need to be identified on a separate checklist in conjunction with evaluative questioning as in Example B. Any evaluative process should have a clear purpose which is clearly defined as in (a), (b) and (c) on page xx.

Some considerations

If you and/or your class have never done Drama or you would like to feel a little more confident with it before beginning, here are some hints before you start.

(a) One of the first things you must establish with your class is a 'stop' signal. Children can get very excited during a drama activity and if it is prolonged the 'stop' signal can be used at any time to break it up with reflection, stillness or discussion. Also as children become more confident with drama experiences they develop increased concentration and become more absorbed in what they are doing. During such times a teacher may need to 'interrupt' the drama with a pause or silence to encourage children to reflect or be guided to the next step of the drama. In these instances the 'stop' signal should be introduced as sensitively as possible so as not to interfere with children's concentration and to enable the drama to continue without interruption to the next stage of development.

Instruments like the tambour, triangle or bell could be used in various ways during the lesson. Signals could be introduced to convey different messages, for example, in group work ringing the triangle quickly could indicate that discussion time is over, slow regular ringing may indicate the working noise level is too high, while a soft rhythmic ring during periods of high concentration may be the signal to look and listen to the teacher while still retaining character or the mood of the drama. If children are required to come to an immediate and/or complete stop the word 'freeze' may be used. This signal requires children to immediately cease whatever movement or process they are engaged in and become 'frozen' in their action as if they were statues. These signals and all other routines must be introduced and practised before engaging in the units.

(b) Establish the space children may use. For example, 'You may use the area to the edge of the carpet', or 'You may use only your personal space'.

(c) Choose shorter/less complex activities at first and progress to more involved ones later. You could even break up an activity and do sections of it over a period of a day. The format of the activities encourage flexibility.

(d) Before beginning specific sections of the activity alert children to the time available for completing it, for example 'You have five minutes for discussion'. Ring a bell when time is up. A sand clock would work for younger children.

(e) The units have been especially designed to keep children to develop social skills to maximise learning experiences. The activities involve children in self-expressive work and in the development of working relationships through partner and small group work. The most effective learning occurs when children engage in partner work especially if they have limited drama experiences. Initially children relate more confidently in a one-to-one situation but partner work helps to develop the more complex skills required for group work.

Turn to the next section for some simple drama activities which you can do with children to help establish rules before you begin the units.

Drama activities for getting started

Activities to develop:
— personal body—space awareness
— recognition of stop/start signals
— partner-work skills

Personal body-space awareness

A Teacher talk: Everyone needs a certain amount of personal space to do things in.
Show how much space you would need to:
— jump up and down
— do sit-ups
— skip with a rope
— write a story on the floor
— eat spaghetti
— stretch out in bed
— tie your shoelaces
— work on a computer

Children mime these as they are called out.

B Teacher talk: Find a space.
Make yourself as large as you can without moving out of your space.
Make yourself as small as you can.
You are a microscopic seed. You slowly begin to send out a tiny shoot.
You are growing very gradually. Stretch slowly towards the sun until you can stretch no further.

C Teacher talk: You are a clam at the bottom of the sea.
Open up very slowly. You are hoping to trap some food. A small fish is close to you. Slam shut quickly to catch it.

D Teacher talk: Imagine you have to paint the inside of a large box while you are standing in it.
The paint and brushes are on the floor in front of you.
Paint the front of the box.
Paint the back. Remember you only have enough room to turn on the spot.
Now paint each side. Be careful not to smudge the paint.

E Teacher talk: Imagine that you are inside a bubble. Float around the room in a clockwise direction.
Keep your personal body-space around you.
If you touch anyone your bubble will burst.

F Teacher talk: Imagine that you are walking on a tight-rope.
Keep your body space around you. If you touch anyone you could fall off.

Start and stop signals

Use a tambour/bell or call out 'freeze' for these activities.
Each time the signal is heard the children stop their activity.

A Ask the children to mime an animal.
Stop their mime with the signal.
Ask children to mime an old person.
Stop their mime with the signal.
Each time the tambour signals, children stop and become different characters.

B Children walk around the room clockwise.
Each time the stop signal is given they stop, count to five and change directions. Repeat this activity each time changing the mode of moving, for example, crawling, hopping.

C Teacher talk: You are a giant clam at the bottom of the sea. Practise opening and closing slowly.
Stop when you hear the signal.

D Teacher talk: Imagine that you are in a bus which is stopping and starting.
When you hear the freeze signal stop.
When you hear the tambour signal start.

Partner-work skills

A Children find a partner. Number each child 1 or 2. Number 1 becomes a mirror, number 2 is the person looking in the mirror. The person looking in the mirror does actions slowly which the mirror imitates. Partners change roles.

B Children move to music.
Call out a body part. Children find a partner and join to the part of the body named and together continue to move to music. Call out another part of the body. Children find another partner and join to the part of the body named.

C Teacher talk: You are a very strange creature with four legs and four arms.
Find a partner and make this creature together.
Show how the creature would move around the room.

D Divide the class into pairs. Each pair has a friendly conversation. When the stop signal is given they continue their talk but turn their conversation into an argument. Every time the signal is given children change the conversation, for example, make friends, argue, and so on.

E Divide the class into pairs. One person is the sculptor and the other is a lump of clay. The sculptor moulds the clay by verbal directions, for example, 'Stretch out your right hand, bend your elbow, kneel . . . '.
Children change roles and repeat the activity.

The environment

The environment: Section A

The indoor environment

Expectations are that children:
- become aware of what is immediately around them
- identify what is made by people

○ **Resources:** Classroom, classroom furniture, equipment, materials
Skills: Observing, describing, reporting, comparing, exploring, questioning, hypothesising
Concepts: Size, big, small, inside, outside, environment

What did you do today?

I visited a classroom. Couldn't find a thing to eat... Lots of strange animals!

1 **Teacher talk:** *Where are we?*
We're in a classroom, aren't we!
What's outside this room?

Encourage children to talk about areas outside the classroom, for example the hall, other rooms, outside walkway, asphalt areas, oval, playground, streets, houses, suburbs, cities, states, country, etc.

2 **Teacher talk:** *The world is a big place, isn't it!*
Imagine how big our classroom environment would be to a very small insect?

Children pretend they are tiny insects. Tell them that they cannot be seen or heard.

3 **Teacher talk:** *Find a spot in the room to rest.*
You've walked a long way.
When you have rested slowly and quietly, explore what is around you.

4 Children sit in the class group and in role as the insect report their observations of the classroom. Remind children that they would need to describe things, since the insect would not know the name of things it saw.

5 Organise children into pairs.
One is the insect who explored the classroom and the other a friend insect who has only seen the outdoors.
Teacher talk: *Tell your friend what you saw inside the classroom.*

○ **Resources:** Classroom or open space, classroom furniture, equipment, materials
Skills: Identifying, presenting
Concepts: People-made (manufactured)

1 Organise children into pairs.
One child becomes an inanimate object. The object must be visible in the classroom.
The other child becomes the user of the object.

2 The partners briefly practise this activity.

3 Each pair then presents their mime to the class who attempt to identify the object.

Resources: Classroom, classroom furniture, equipment, materials
Skills: Questioning, inferring, describing, hypothesising
Concepts: Living, non-living things, growth

1 Organise children into pairs.
Teacher talk: Pretend the classroom is a jungle and you are explorers.
It is a strange jungle because it does not have things that grow.

Before children begin the activity ask them what they would expect to find in a jungle. Make comparisons between living things and inanimate objects.

2 *Teacher talk: As you explore talk about each discovery with your partner.*
What is it?
Is it a growing thing? How do you know?
Does it move?

3 Have children bring back one object from the jungle and describe it to the class.
Encourage children to describe their object and to hypothesise how it was made and what was used to make it.

Resources: Classroom, classroom furniture, equipment, materials, writing paper, pencils
Skills: Discussing, listing, inferring
Concepts: Natural, people-made

Activities (a) and (b) have a follow-through theme and can be taught in sequence or alone.

(a)
1 Children choose one object from the classroom and bring it back to the class group.
Teacher talk: You are a worker who makes things like the one you have in your hand.
Pretend to make an object just like it.
What materials will you need?

2 Discuss with the whole group what kind of materials might be needed for different objects.
Each child writes a list of materials needed.

3 *Teacher talk: Get your (imaginary) materials ready and make your object.*

4 Discuss the finished products.
Use the discussion to determine whether any natural materials were needed for making the object (for example wood).

○
□ **Resources:** Classroom, classroom furniture, equipment, materials
Skills: Sorting, grouping, categorising, discussing
Concepts: Manufacture, environment, cause and effect

(b)

1 In the class group, question children specifically about where their particular object was made.
   Teacher talk: Where was your object made?
   Were all the objects made in the same place?
   Would a chair be made in the same place as a pencil?
2 Children group with others whose objects were made in the same place.
3 *Teacher talk: With your group build an environment to make your object in.*
   (Before beginning this activity make rules about what can be used for construction, for example chairs, blocks, mats, etc.)
4 When children have completed their environment, in their groups they discuss their roles as workers in that environment, that is, what kind of work they do and what they will be involved in making, etc.).
5 Have children make their objects in their working environment.

The outdoor environment
Expectations are that children:
• explore the outdoor school environment
• observe what is natural

○
□ **Resources:** Outdoor areas, writing pads, pencils, bell or tambour
Skills: Exploring, discovering, predicting, discussing, recording, reporting
Concepts: Senses, planets

1 Choose an outdoor area in which to begin this activity (for example asphalt area).
   Set boundaries by clearly defining how much of the area children should use.
   Teacher talk: Pretend you are a visitor from another planet. You have been sent on a mission to discover what is on earth.

   Children close their eyes and imagine they have just landed in their spaceship and think of what they will do when they open their eyes.
   Children open their eyes and discuss their plans.
2 *Teacher talk: What will you need to take with you from the spaceship?*
   Encourage children to offer suggestions of imaginary items which should include a real writing pad and pencil.
3 Have children begin their exploration of the designated area and record their findings. Suggest that their writing may differ from that of earth people.

Encourage children to use their five senses for exploration as everything is new and different from their own planet. Children discuss their findings with each other as they explore.

4 At a given signal (for example bell), children return to their spaceship.
Teacher talk: *It is time for you to return to your planet. Remember you can breathe earth air only for a short time.*

Children prepare for take-off and begin the countdown 10-9-8...

5 Have everyone close their eyes and imagine they are flying through space to their home planet.
Teacher talk: *Pretend you have arrived back home on your planet.*
You are excited about what you have found out.
Quickly go to the palace to tell your leader of your discoveries.

At this stage the teacher may assume the role of the leader. Encourage the children to greet you accordingly and share their findings.
(This sequence of activities may be repeated with more than one area of the school, for example oval, garden, grassy area.)

Resources: Outdoor areas
Skills: Discussing, observing, exploring, categorising, questioning
Concepts: People-made, natural, senses, living, non-living

1 Choose an outdoor working area where there are people-made things (buildings, play equipment) and natural things (trees, soil, flowers).
Organise children into groups of four or five.
2 Have children walk around in groups using their senses to explore the area. Encourage children to talk to each other about their sensory findings (for example, 'This part of the building feels very rough.' or 'This plant smells very sweet.').
3 In their groups children discuss their observations. Children should reflect on whether things are made by people or are natural things.
4 Each group decides to become one of the things they have observed (for example a door, a fence, a tree). They practise making with their bodies the thing they have decided on.
5 Each group presents their body structure to the class. Others guess what it is.
Encourage children to ask appropriate questions (for example, 'Is it made by people?' 'Is it a living thing?').

Resources: Outdoor areas, pencils, writing pads

Skills: Hypothesising, discussing, categorising, decision-making

Concepts: Time (before, after), natural, people-made, modification, change

1 **Teacher talk:** Close your eyes and imagine what this land looked like before the school was built. What was on the basketball court?
Did the oval always look like that?
What was here before the buildings were built?

Children discuss.

2 **Teacher talk:** Pretend you are workers standing on this land. You have been asked to begin building the school.
Where will you begin?
What will you do first?

Children discuss.

3 Organise children into teams of workers (for example, bricklayers, landscapers, painters, tractor drivers).
Each team decides what job they will do, (for example build the office, gym, level the oval, plant seeds, etc.) and list what materials they will need.

4 **Teacher talk:** Are you ready, workers?
Gather your tools and materials and get to work.

5 As the groups work walk around and enquire on progress and difficulties encountered.

6 Children then talk about their experiences with the whole class.
Encourage children to say whether materials used were entirely people-made or included natural materials.

Using the environment for leisure and work

Expectations are that children:
- become aware that the environment is used for leisure
- become aware that the environment is used for work
- make comparisons between natural and people-made environments

Resources: Pictures of hills, valleys, rivers, seas, workers in the natural environment

Skills: Decision-making, discussing, planning, identifying, reporting

Concepts: Needs, modification, preservation, causality, change

1 **Teacher talk:** Pretend you are going away on holidays with a friend.
Which of these places would you like to visit?

Show pictures of the beach, sea, rivers, hills, etc.
Children partner someone who has chosen the same holiday.

2 **Teacher talk:** What will you need to take with you on the holiday?
Where are you going to stay, a tent/motel/caravan?

Children discuss with their friend.

Encourage children to think about the weather and the kind of activities they will be doing on their holiday.

As children plan their holiday walk around, ask questions and offer advice where appropriate.

3 Children pack for their holiday and board their mode of transport (for example, car, bicycle, airplane, ship).
Teacher talk: *Have you packed everything you need? Are you ready? Off you go!*

Have children close their eyes and imagine their journey, then act it out.

4 On arrival children unpack their equipment and act out the holiday activities.

5 Children return home and share their holiday news with other friends.
Organise children to share with another couple.

6 Each child draws a 'photo' of themselves at the place they visited.

7 Display the completed pictures.
Encourage children to comment on what is happening in each picture (that is how each person used the environment). Also ask children to identify the natural environment and any changes which they think have been made by people (for example, did anyone make the river, hillside; did someone make the path through the mountains?).

○ **Resources:** Classroom or open space, poster paper, paper and pencils, textas
Skills: Categorising, sorting, grouping, identifying, comparing, presenting
Concepts: Occupations, natural, people-made, working environment, spatial terms (indoor, outdoor)

1 Have children name their parents' jobs. List these on a poster.

2 In their personal space children mime one of the occupations listed.

3 Some children then mime their chosen occupation to the class. The class guess what activity is being performed.
Also have children suggest whether the activity is being performed in a natural or people-made setting.

4 Organise children into same occupation groups.
Have them discuss the kind of environment they work in.
Teacher talk: *What kinds of things do you have in your working environment (for example office—chair, phone, desk)? Is it an indoor or outdoor job?*

In their groups children write a list of things which make up their environment.

5 Groups of children make a tableau of their working environment by becoming the things they have listed.

6 Children present their group work to others.
Encourage the audience to comment on aspects of the work environment and make comparisons between natural and people-made environments.

Resources: Pictures of natural environments

Skills: Decision-making, defining, reporting, exploring, discussing

Concepts: Natural, change, modification, causality

1 *Teacher talk: You are a person who works in a natural environment.*
Choose one of these environments to work in, for example:
Coast   Valley   River   Jungle   Forest Desert
(fisherman) (farmer) (boat owner) (road-builder) (ranger) (miner)

2 Organise children into groups according to their choice of environment.
Each group decides what work they do in their environment.

3 (Before children begin organise a working space for each group and have them explore their work environment.)
Teacher talk: What do you see?
What kinds of things are around you?
Remember that in the natural environment nothing has been changed or made by people.

4 The leader representing each group reports to the class on what the exploration revealed.

5 Groups plan the kind of work they will do in their natural environment.
Teacher talk: What will you need to do your work?
What will you need to take with you (for example miner— shovels, bucket, rope)?
Get your things ready.

6 Groups improvise working in the natural environment using things brought with them.

7 *Teacher talk: It's now the end of the day!*
You are very tired. Pack up, it's time to go home.
Come and sit by me and tell me about your day.

Encourage children to think about whether their work activities had made any changes to their environment.

Resources: Open space
Skills: Suggesting, defining, comparing
Concepts: Work, leisure

1 **Teacher talk:** Let's go on an outing for the day.
Where would you like to go?

Children make suggestions, for example the park, the beach, the city, etc.
(Choose the most popular place to visit with the whole group.)
Teacher talk: Who are you going with?
(Have children choose friends, mum and dad, and so on, to go with.)
Close your eyes. When you open them again you will be in the city.

2 Have children improvise the scene in their groups.
Teacher talk: I love the city. There are so many things to look at.
Look, what's that in the shop window?

3 **Teacher talk:** It's been a long day. It's time to go home.
Close your eyes and imagine you are back home.

Ask children what they were doing in the city (park, beach or whatever).
Have children say whether theirs was a work or leisure activity.

4 **Teacher talk:** Were there other people in the city?
What were they doing in the city?

Children determine whether work activities can occur at the same time as leisure activities in the same environment.

Resources: Open space
Skills: Exploring, describing, reporting
Concepts: Natural, people-made, spatial terms (underneath, on top)

Activities (a) and (b) have a follow-through theme and can be taught in sequence or alone.

(a)

1 **Teacher talk:** Let's pretend that the world is flat and shaped like a square.
One half of the world is natural and the other half is people-made.
Divide the space into natural and people-made.

2 **Teacher talk:** We are creatures living underneath the flat world.
Nothing much happens underneath the world.
Let's go and see what's on top.
Sssh, we don't want people to know we're snooping around!

Divide the class into two groups. One group's task is to explore the natural world and the other is to explore the people-made world.

3 As children explore encourage them to react to what they see by whispering to each other and making comments.

4 **Teacher talk:** Ssh, I think I hear someone coming.
Quick, we'd better go back to our world.

5 The two groups sit opposite each other and share their findings.

Resources: Open space, party lunch, letter of invitation, bag filled with natural and people-made items, bell, costume for 'Leader'.
Skills: Sorting, describing, valuing, suggesting, exploring
Concepts: Natural foods, natural, people-made

(b)

1 **Teacher talk:** *I found this letter on my desk this morning. It's addressed to: The creatures who live underneath my square flat world.*
This is what it says:

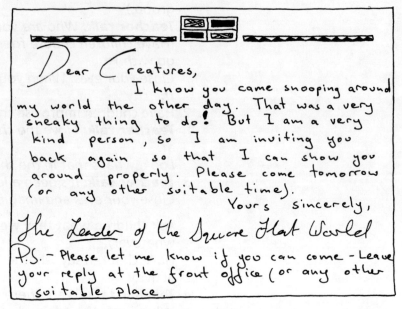

> Dear Creatures,
>   I know you came snooping around my world the other day. That was a very sneaky thing to do! But I am a very kind person, so I am inviting you back again so that I can show you around properly. Please come tomorrow (or any other suitable time).
>   Yours sincerely,
> The Leader of the Square Flat World
> P.S. — Please let me know if you can come — Leave your reply at the front office (or any other suitable place.

2 The letter should elicit all kinds of reactions from complete belief in the letter to incredulity. However, the success of the activity is dependent on the children's imaginations and the teacher's determination to make it credible.

3 Have the class help draft out a reply to the letter, for example:
Dear Leader of the Square Flat World,
Thank you for your invitation. We would like to come and see your world again. We are sorry for coming without permission. We will come tomorrow at noon.
Yours sincerely,
The creatures Who Live Underneath Your Flat Square World.

4 The next day (or whatever time is agreed on) the children visit the flat world.
Teacher talk: *I wonder where the leader is?*
What shall we do while we're waiting?

Encourage children to make suggestions to do with exploring the place.

5 While children carry out some of the suggestions the Leader of the Square Flat World* arrives.
(*The Leader's arrival has been arranged prior to the beginning of this activity. The character could wear a suitable costume. The person in role could be one of the parents, office staff or another teacher, in fact, anyone who is confident enough.)

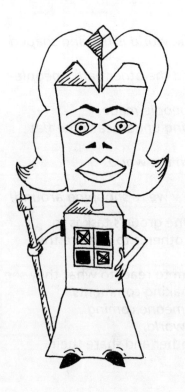

Children should be unaware of the planning that has occurred. When the Leader arrives be prepared for any number of responses.

Be prepared for anything!

6   The Leader is mildly annoyed because children are exploring without waiting for her arrival.

Leader: What impatient creatures you are! I did say that I was going to show you around.

It's important that I explain natural and people-made things properly.

Now please sit down and listen

(Some of the children at this stage, may be feeling quite overwhelmed).

7   The Leader produces an enormous bag in which there are numerous items, some natural and some people-made.

Leader: I will tell you which part of my world these things come from.

Teacher talk: *But we already know what people-made and natural things are.*

The Leader is taken aback and asks children if this is so.

8   As each thing is pulled out of the bag by the Leader a child offers to put it on the side of the world in which it belongs.

9   When all the objects have been placed correctly the Leader tells the children how pleased she is with them for being so clever.

Leader: Because you are so clever you must share lunch with me.

10 On a given signal the door opens and the Leader's servants (parent helpers) carry in plates of food*: some natural (apples, carrots, celery, etc.) and some people-made from natural things (cakes, bread and butter, popcorn, etc.).

(*This party lunch has of course been carefully planned and organised without the children's knowledge.)

11 As children enjoy the party atmosphere the Leader and the teacher could wander around talking about the different foods, until eventually the Leader leaves unnoticed (if possible).

Changing the natural environment

Expectations are that children:

- develop an awareness of changes made to our natural environment
- become aware that some changes are made to satisfy people's needs

Resources: Open space, Aboriginal Dreaming stories, pictures of natural settings.

Skills: Discussing, planning, inferring, questioning

Concepts: Changes, modification

1 Read some Aboriginal Dreaming stories. Discuss.
2 *Teacher talk: Pretend you have magical powers. You can do things which other people can't. You can make a natural environment.*

Show pictures of natural settings and discuss.
3 Have children write an imaginative story about how they would make a natural environment. Children say what would be part of their environment before they begin.
4 Children read their completed stories to the class.

5 Select some of the stories for children to act out in groups. In groups children discuss, plan, then improvise their stories.
6 Each group presents their story to the class.
7 The class asks questions and gives feedback about each performance.
Question children specifically as to what was used to make particular environments (for example water, soil, seeds, etc.).
Teacher talk: What happened to the seeds? Did they all grow? What did they grow into?

Resources: Open space, Aboriginal Dreaming stories

Skills: Grouping, identifying, discussing, recalling, predicting

Concepts: Causality, weather, elements, eco-system, needs, co-operation

1 Read some Aboriginal Dreaming stories.
Teacher talk: Pretend you are something in the natural environment. What can you be?

Suggest that children can be an animal, plant or element (that is water, wind, rain, sun, etc.)
2 *Teacher talk: Find your own space in the bush and become part of the natural environment.*
After the children have established their role organise them into the categories (animal, plant and element) with a leader for each group.

3 Explain that now they are to become the spirit of the animal, plant or element.
Impress upon them that they are not the animal, plant or element itself but the spirit which takes care of them and that it is the co-operation between the spirits which makes the bush a good safe environment to be in.

4 Children introduce themselves individually and say what their job is, for example:
'I am the spirit of the trees and I keep them safe and happy in the bush.'
or
'I am the spirit of water and I make sure that all the waterholes are filled for the animals.'
or
'I am the spirit of the kangaroos and I make sure that we do not eat all the grasses so that there is enough food for other animals.'

5 Groups improvise the bush environment—acting out what happens daily in the bush (for example it rains, the sun shines, trees grow, animals eat, etc.).

Resources: Open space
Skills: Discussing, predicting, inferring
Concepts: Eco-system, early settlers, needs, modification and causality

1 Choose some children to be early settler families. Others represent the Australian bush.

2 ***Teacher talk:*** *The people have come a long way to make a home for themselves.*
Show what happens when they come into the bush.
What do they do?
What do the animals do?
What happens to the environment?
The children act out what happens in the scene.

3 After the improvisation children discuss what happened. Encourage them to discuss their feelings as representatives of the bush and as the early settler families.
Ask questions such as:
Did the people change the environment?
How? Did they need to do that? Why?
How do you think the bush creatures felt?
Did they like the changes?

Resources: Open space
Skills: Discussing, suggesting, inferring, hypothesising
Concepts: Causality, eco-system, modification

1 Tell the children that they are going to make up a story in which there are groups of pine trees, birds, and workers.
Teacher talk: *What could the story be about?*

Children make suggestions. Encourage children to think of a setting where all of these characters come together.

2 Organise children into groups of birds, trees and workers. Have them improvise what happens when they come together.

3 In the class discuss what happened. Question children specifically to determine whether any changes were made to the environment, for example:
What did the workers do (plant trees or chop them down)?
Was the environment changed as a result?
What do you think happened to the trees, birds, etc.?

○ **Resources:** Classroom,
□ drama blocks, desks,
chairs, mats, boxes, etc.
Skills: Categorising,
sorting, grouping,
discussing, hypothesising,
suggesting, defining
Concepts: Needs, wants

I know white suits you, but I think it looked better on the elephant.

1 ***Teacher talk:*** *Have you ever been in a furniture shop?*
What kinds of things are in there?
(Children offer suggestions.)
I would like you to make a furniture shop.
2 Children set up shop using available equipment as props, for example boxes, drama blocks, chairs, etc.
Teacher talk: *I am the manager and I'm going to inspect what you're selling!*
3 Have children stand by different bits of 'furniture' as you move to each in the role of the manager.
Teacher talk: *What is this? What is it made of (for example plastic, wood, etc.)?*
This doesn't belong here, it goes in a washing machine shop.
4 In role of the manager call a meeting of the people who work in the shop.
Teacher talk: *I've noticed that some things in the shop are made of wood (or straw, iron, etc.).*
Are these things people need?
Or are these things people want?

Discuss with the group.
5 ***Teacher talk:*** *Pretend you are the voice of something in the shop.*
Have children become an object in the shop. Ask some what they are and if any part of them is made of wood.
Enquire as to where the wood came from. Encourage children to hypothesise about the wood's former environment.

Appreciation of our natural environment

Expectations are that children:
• develop an awareness of the beauty and importance of natural things in their lives
• recognise the importance of respecting the natural environment and using it appropriately

Resources: Open space/classroom, drama blocks, mats, tables and chairs
Skills: Appreciating, valuing, categorising, observing, discussing
Concepts: Aesthetics, identification of criteria

1 Have children talk about things that they think are beautiful. Children give reasons for choices, that is why these things are a thing of beauty and therefore appreciated by them.
2 In the class group, children make a list of the beautiful things discussed. Children help put them into natural or people-made categories.
3 Ask children to make an environment, using classroom equipment/furniture, where these beautiful things can be put on display.
4 Children display the imaginary items and group them as natural or people-made things.
5 In pairs children become visitors to the exhibition. Encourage children to talk about what they see to their partners.
6 Have children share their observations with the class.

Resources: Open space/classroom, sheet of paper, textas
Skills: Categorising, grouping, valuing, labelling, recording, valuing, reflecting
Concepts: Eco-system, environmental ethics, aesthetics

I'd give anything for a bit of sunshine...

Oh, it would absolutely ruin me!

1 Ask children to imagine that they are something beautiful which has been put on display in a gallery. Children say what they are and where they come from or where they belong, for example: a car—I belong in a garage, a flower—I belong in a back yard
2 Encourage children to imagine that their thing can talk and has feelings.
   *Teacher talk: You have been standing very still all day so that people can admire and look at you.
   Now everyone has gone home.
   How do you feel about being on display?
   Do you ever think about where you come from?
   Do you think about the things you could do before?*

   Encourage children to make comments and discuss.
3 Some children become objects in a gallery, others become visitors. Before visitors arrive each object is to be clearly labelled, for example: tree—former home, the hills. Encourage the visitors to read the labels and to discuss what they see with others.
4 *Teacher talk: The visitors have gone home now.
   The things on display can relax.
   Talk to each other about how you feel.*

   Encourage children to think about how they would feel if they had been put in a place where they could do nothing but be looked at.

○ **Resources:** Open space
Skills: Discussing, describing
Concepts: Growth, plant life, (Maths: sequence, size, long, small)

1 In pairs children become vegetable or fruit plants in a garden. Firstly have children discuss what they would look like, that is what parts make up their plant—roots, leaves, fruit and so on.
2 With a partner children become the plant. Remind children that they are part of the same plant. Encourage them to think about size and different parts of the plant, and to show these with their body shape.
3 Walk around the garden and make comments about the different plants.
Teacher talk: I can see this plant has very long roots. I wonder if it has any fruit on it!

○ **Resources:** Open space, books on plants, air/water
Skills: Discussing, inferring, researching
Concepts: Ecosystem, natural resources, growth

1 *Teacher talk: Why are plants important to us? What do plants need to grow?*

Children research and discuss.
2 Choose children to become trees, seeds, rain, falling leaves, wind, earthworms, sunlight, night and day and so on.
3 As each character is mentioned in the following story children act out their roles.
*Teacher talk: You are a seed resting on a grassy field.
The wind comes along and blows you gently about.
Then it gets stronger and carries you far away to another part of the land.
It is night time and you are feeling very cold.
Gentle rain begins to fall on you and you become wet.
The soil you are resting on is very soft and mushy.
You feel yourself sinking softly into the ground.
The wind blows some more but it can no longer move you.
You are stuck in the mud.
You are tired and you fall asleep for a long time.
Daylight comes, the sun shines warmly around.
You begin to feel warm.
You slowly reach out a little green shoot towards the sun.
You slowly throw out another little shoot into the soil.
You are now beginning to grow.*

Continue in this way, making use of all the characters, for example more rain, more sun, the earthworms making the soil healthy and so on.

Environment activities across the curriculum

Language

Write a story as an insect being trapped inside a human's house.

Write shape stories, that is a story about a tree inside a tree shape.

Write descriptions of objects made by people.

Make a list of questions to ask a tree/animal about changes to the natural environment.

Write stories about going on journeys to visit:
—another planet
—a jungle
—the land of insects (bugs, animals).

Write a vocabulary list for holiday pictures. Place descriptive word-cards on or around the scene.

Tell well-known stories; children add environmental sounds to the story (for example wind blowing, leaves rustling, water dripping).

Make a class book telling how we appreciate our environment through our senses (touch, smell, hearing, etc.).

Play 'What am I?' using natural things as the theme.

Read stories set in the natural environment.

Read a story—write down all the things in it that belong to the natural environment.

Mathematics

Measure and weigh people-made objects—is the size an indication of how heavy things are?

Collect leaves, use them to sort and pattern. How many different criteria can you use to sort them?

Look for creatures within a defined natural setting. How many do you see? Make a graph showing number, kind and size of creatures.

Measure leaf and plant growth. Monitor growth on a chart.

Find symmetry in nature.

Section off a small area (one metre square) of garden/grass. Count the number of flowers in each. Sort them into categories.

Estimate the width of a tree trunk—find an arbitrary measure to check accuracy.

Measure the distance between play equipment in the playground.

Society
Find out about famous explorers. What lands did they travel to?
Compare city life and country life.
Draw a map of the local area—walk around the neighbourhood and mark things on the map as you discover them, for example hall, park, hotel, etc.
Walk around the neighbourhood and look at people's gardens. Are things growing in a natural setting?
Have a photo exhibition showing leisure activities; write captions for each.
Invite parents in to talk about their work environment.
Look at pictures of different environments. What kinds of living things might you find in each.
Draw a home for a desert, mountain, sea environment.

Science
Collect things to observe from the natural environment—categorise into living and non-living; define how they relate to each other. Blindfolded, use the sense of smell to identify natural/manufactured things.
Observe small creatures in their natural environment. Record your findings.
Place bread scraps outside the window. What kind of creatures are attracted. Keep a record of the visits.

Environment
In a blank map of your country place cut-outs of living things (animals, plants, people). What are there more of? Discuss, re-arrange to show correct proportion.
Visit your community centre. What information can you find about your area?
Display products which contain natural materials. Show their journey in pictures from the natural environment to the final product.
Draw a map of an imaginary land showing features of our natural environment (for example river, mountains, lakes, valleys, plains, hills, oceans), then photocopy. Show changes made by people in the second copy. Compare the two.
Use paper and crayons to make rubbings of the patterns in nature, for example bark, wood.
Make miniature gardens. Monitor conditions for growth.
Use natural materials to make a 'dry' garden.

Art
Paint a garden scene as seen through the eyes of a small

insect. Draw/cut out pictures of insects, paste them on the scene.

Make a poster collage of things collected in the natural environment.

Draw a scene showing what the land looked like before the school was built. Draw another one to show what it looks like now.

Have a photo exhibition showing the same natural environment in different seasons.

Place paper on something in the natural environment, rub over with crayon to make a print. Display on a poster.

Music

Find information about musical instruments made from natural materials, for example violin, drums, piano, etc.

Compose an environmental song using voices and natural things (for example leaves, twigs, water) to depict sounds such as wind, rain, etc.

Tape record it.

Health

Prepare a menu of natural foods.

Keep a record of foods eaten by children for lunch over a week. How is each prepared; which are eaten in their natural state?

Adopt a pet rock; care for it for a week, then return it to the natural environment.

Sit outdoors. Listen to the sounds around you—identify them.

Make a tape of environmental sounds. Identify each. How do you feel when you listen to different sounds?

Walk outdoors and use your senses to pick up indications of changes in the weather.

Discuss weather and our reactions to it. Make a chart of weather conditions and draw pictures of clothing appropriate for each day.

Collect seeds from the fruit and vegetables you eat over a period of time. Dry in the sun and plant.

Describe fruit and vegetables by touch and smell.

Technology

Design and make out of scrap materials a machine which could be used by insects to:

   —protect them from people's feet

   —clean off insecticide from vegetables they eat

   —an alarm to warn them when humans are coming.

Construct a city using cartons and scrap materials.
Find out about machines used in work places; categorise
according to the most appropriate work places for them, for
example:
    —conveyer belt—factories
    —word processor—office
Make a periscope to explore the natural environment. Use
two mirrors, a shoebox, masking tape, glue, scissors.

The environment: Section B

Air all around us

Expectations are that children:
- come to the understanding that air is all around us
- identify indicators which show that air is present
- develop an awareness of the composition of air

Resources: Classroom, small box with lid, balloons
Skills: Inferring, questioning, hypothesising
Concepts: Air is all around, atmosphere, air fills up space; spatial terms: front, behind, above, below, inside, outside

1 Children sit in a circle and pass around an empty sealed box and reflect on what might be inside.
  Teacher talk: *The box is full of something. You can't touch it, but you can sometimes feel it. What do you think it might be?*
2 Have children stand in their personal space and touch the space all around them (in front, behind, above, below, etc.).
  Teacher talk: *Can you feel anything? What is in the box that is also around you? (air)*

Resources: Open space, balloons, 'floating' music
Skills: Observing, comparing, experimenting, hypothesising
Concepts: Tiny, inside/outside, floating, expansion

1 Children pretend they are balloons, making themselves very tiny and then expanding slowly as they fill with air.
2 The balloons float about in the air.
  Teacher talk: *Is the air inside or outside keeping you afloat? How do you know?*
3 Experiment with real balloons. Indoors—observe the movement of balloons. Have children compare this with their own movements as balloons. Outdoors—observe the balloons again and make comparisons and conclusions. Remove air from the balloons both indoors and outdoors—what happens?
4 Dramatise the movement of balloons:
  (a) before inflation
  (b) filling with air
  (c) floating in the air
  (d) rapidly deflating.
  Perform the stages of balloon movement to music.

Resources: Classroom or open space, large sheet of paper, textas
Skills: Observing, discussing, questioning, inferring, comparing
Concepts: Wind power, expansion, movement of air

1 Children find a partner—one becomes a balloon, the other inflates the balloon. An extended open hand represents the air outlet. One partner blows into the hand to inflate the balloon.
2 When the balloons are full of air partners pat them gently to move them in the air around the room. Encourage the balloons to move as they are guided.

3 **Teacher talk:** *Where did the air to blow up the balloons come from?*
Could you feel the air in your hand when you were being blown up?
Can you feel the air around you now in the same way? Why/why not?

Have children blow into their own hands and feel the air.
Teacher talk: *Which did you feel most, the air blown into your hand or the air around you? Why?*

4 Have children identify times when they have felt air.
Teacher talk: *What were you doing? What was happening around you?*

Half the class become balloons again, the others observe.
Have the balloons fill with air but remain still.
Teacher talk: *The balloons are full of air but they are not floating. Why?*
What would happen if the room was windy?

Resources: Large space, poster paper, textas
Skills: Observing, comparing, hypothesising, forming conclusions
Concepts: Wind power, insulation, movement, stillness

1 **Teacher talk:** *Let's go on a journey!*
Where shall we go (the seaside, the city, the country, etc.)?
It's a cold windy day, wear something warm!

The class chooses a place to visit. Ask children to suggest appropriate clothing to wear and the purpose of the clothing.
Children put on the clothing and visit the chosen scene.
During the visit ask children what they can see and what they are doing.
Suggest activities appropriate to the scene.

2 Back in the class group, children describe the scene visited, (for example, at the seaside: a sailboat, people playing with beach balls, sand, sea, trees, umbrellas, etc.).
List on a large sheet.

3 Individuals choose from the list and mime or figurate, (for example a sailboat or a person playing). Remind children to react appropriately to a very strong wind. Use the freeze signal intermittently to create a tableau, of stillness and movement within the improvisation.

4 During the periods of stillness call out one or two items listed. Children representing these show how they react to the force of the wind.
Cease movement by repeating the freeze signal.

5 In the class group, discuss if there would still be movement in some things if there was no wind (for example a sailboat, a flag, a person).

6 Repeat the improvisation firstly with wind, then without. Children make comparisons between the two.

Resources: Classroom, letter from an alien, poster paper, textas
Skills: Observing, questioning, investigating, making conclusions, hypothesising
Concepts: Air fills up space, displacement of air, composition of air; spatial terms: around, on top, in, inside, under

(a)

1 **Teacher talk:** *Air is all around us!*
It is in, under and on top of things.
We know that, don't we!
But here's a letter from someone who doesn't know much about air at all.

2 Read letter:

Discuss the letter. Tell children that they will go on a hunt for air.
Children suggest where it could be and what they could use for 'air catching' equipment.
Have children prepare the imaginary equipment.
Teacher talk: *Right, let's go!*
Is it under the table? In this container?
Inside the cupboard/drawers?
Can air be inside food, plants, soil, etc.?

Examine a wide variety of things to determine whether air is contained inside things, (for example food, sponges).

3 Children return to the class group and list things seen which take up space that air would otherwise have taken up. Guide children to the understanding that air fills up space and can be displaced.

4 Begin a class letter to the Alien from Ria responding to the first question.
'In what places do you have air?'

Activities (a) and (b) have a follow-through theme and can be taught in sequence or alone.

Resources: Classroom and large open space, alien's letter (as above), cardboard stencil outline of sunglasses, coloured cellophane, scissors, glue, cardboard placards (for example, for a class of 25:nitrogen gas (19 placards), oxygen gas (5 placards), other gases (1 placard))
Skills: Observing, hypothesising, forming conclusions, recording
Concepts: Composition of air, air gases

(b)

1 *Teacher talk: Can we tell the alien what air is made of?*
We can't see it, smell it or touch it.
Maybe some magic glasses will help!
2 Children make sunglasses from a stencil shape using coloured cellophane for the glass section.
3 The class then goes to another room where cardboard placards with the names of air gases have been placed prior to the lesson.
Children enter wearing glasses and 'see' the air (that is the placards).
Teacher talk: Look, what's this? I think it must be air.
4 Children choose a placard each, then sit in a circle.
Teacher talk: What do you think the air is made up of?
Which gas is there more of?
Who knows what gas we breathe?
5 Children become air and say the word on their card with wind-like voices as they float around the room. Back in the classroom complete the letter to the Alien from Ria.

Resources: Large space
Skills: Discussing, presenting
Concepts: Atmosphere, air movement, weather warm, cold, wet dry

1 *Teacher talk: What's the air around the Earth called?*
It protects us from the sun and keeps us warm at night just like a blanket.
Let's see if we can make a blanket around the Earth.
2 Children form a circle.
Narrate the following as children perform appropriate body actions:
Air is always moving, around the Earth.
Air moves in lots of different ways, in the atmosphere.
Sometimes air is warm.
Sometimes air is cold.
Sometimes it is wet.
Sometimes it is dry.
Moving air helps to make our weather.
3 Discuss the experience, then tell children that they will act out another part of the 'air story'.
Children become the following 'characters':
The land, the sea, the sun, air, (groups of children could represent each character).
4 Children say who they are and in their chosen roles act out the following story:
The sun warms the land.
The sun warms the sea.
The land and the sea warm the cold air.
The air becomes warm and light and floats up, up, up, high in the atmosphere.
The warm air has left a space.
The cold air rushes in to fill that space.

The warm air gets higher and higher; the higher it goes the colder it gets.
When the air is cold it comes down close to the land again.
Then the story happens all over again.

Repeat the story and improvisation.

Breathing and living

Expectations are that children:
- understand that without air we cannot survive
- become aware that all living things take in air
- have an understanding of the breathing cycle

Resources: Open space
Skills: Inferring, investigating, hypothesising
Concepts: The breathing cycle, oxygen, survival needs

Activities (a) and (b) have a follow-through theme and can be taught in sequence or alone.

(a)
1 Discuss and list what is necessary for our survival.
   Teacher talk: *How important is food/air?*
   Let's find out!
2 Children pretend they are in a pool demonstrating swimming strokes.
   Teacher talk: *Who can swim the breast-stroke/butterfly?*
   What can you do under water?
   For how long can you stay underwater?
   Let's see?

Children hold their breath and dive in the water. Count out the seconds children are underwater. Some children may not come up for breath at the appropriate time. Ask them to reflect what might have happened in real water.

3 Children pretend they are deep-sea divers looking for sunken treasure.
   Teacher talk: What will you need to take with you?
   Is there anything you can take to help you stay in the water longer?

   In small groups children discuss what they will need, prepare imaginary equipment and begin their underwater journey. (Have children reflect on where they will go and what they will dive from before they begin).

4 Groups return and share their experiences with the class.
   Teacher talk: What did you see (plants, sea-creatures)?
   How were you breathing?
   Were other things breathing in the water?
   How?

   Discuss.
   Have children reflect on:
   (a) What they would do if something went wrong with their air tank.
   (b) What happens to sea plants and creatures out of water.

○ **Resources:** Classroom,
□ furniture and equipment, pictures of plants, animals/people in underwater, city and country environments; large sheet of paper, textas/pencils
Skills: Observing, inferring, identifying, hypothesising, discussing
Concepts: Living things need air, breathing, needs

(b)

1 Look at pictures of land environments. Identify and write on a sheet the living things in each environment.
   Teacher talk: Does each environment have air?
   How do you know?
   What do living things need to stay alive?

2 Divide children into groups representative of different environments, for example underwater, city, country, desert. Have children make their environment using classroom furniture and equipment.

3 When the environments are completed each child takes on the role of a living thing from the list and becomes part of the environment. Walk around to each group questioning to determine their understanding of how different living things need air.
   Teacher talk: Who/what are you?
   What helps you to live?
   How do you get your food/water/air?

4 Children return to the class group to share their experiences.
   Teacher talk: Do all living things breathe?
   What about water creatures?
   Show pictures of different sea creatures including dolphins, whales, crabs, turtles, etc. Children become sea creatures moving in their natural environment. Encourage children to visualise how and what the sea creature would do in their environment.

5 Assume the role of diver. Tell children that you are coming down to study the sea environment. Question individuals as you move among them.
Teacher talk: What kind of fish are you?
How do you move?
Where do you get your energy from?
What do you need to stay alive?

6 In the class group children reflect on their experiences and make conclusions.
Teacher talk: Is there air in the water?
Why do I need an air tank if there is air in the water?

7 Look at pictures of sea creatures in underwater environments, or fish in aquariums. Have children determine whether the fish are breathing.
Have children suggest why people cannot breathe in water and fish can.

Resources: Open space, blue, green, red coloured streamers, reference books on air/breathing
Skills: Inferring, hypothesising, researching, making conclusions
Concepts: Breathing cycle, oxygen, carbon dioxide

1 *Teacher talk: Do living things breathe the same gases from the air?*
Why? Why not?
Do all living things breathe in the same way?
Let's see if we can find out!

Children read books on living things, their survival needs and their use of air.

2 Ask children to help you tell the breathing cycle story. Choose children to become plants, animals, people, oxygen, carbon dioxide.
Children representing the air carry coloured streamers, for example:
—oxygen—blue streamer
—carbon dioxide—green streamer
—other gases—red streamer

3 Children act out the story as it is narrated.
Pace it so that children have enough time to think about what is happening.
Teacher talk: Once upon a time there was a beautiful planet called Earth.
The people, the animals and plants lived happily together.
The air was clean and fresh.
It filled up all the space it could find.
(The air characters move around the others waving their streamers.)
The people were healthy and strong.
They breathed in oxygen from the air.
(The oxygen characters move to the people.)
And then the people breathed out carbon dioxide—the air they didn't need!

(Children with the green streamers representing carbon dioxide move away from the people.)
The animals were healthy and strong too.
They breathed in oxygen from the air.
And breathed out the carbon dioxide they didn't need.
Plants need carbon dioxide to live.
So they used the carbon dioxide in the air.
Then the plants breathed out oxygen for the people and animals.
Every moment of every day, people breathed in the oxygen;
people breathed out carbon dioxide;
plants took in carbon dioxide;
plants breathed out oxygen;
animals breathed in oxygen;
animals breathed out carbon dioxide.
The people and animals and plants lived
happily together until something happened to the air.
4 Discuss what might have happened to the air and what would happen to living things as a result of polluted air.

○ **Resources:** Open space
□ **Skills:** Discussing, hypothesising, problem-
△ solving, predicting, comparing
Concepts: Growth, cause and effect; needs, survival, pollution, eco-system

1 Have children make up a story in which there are:
—crop farmers
—bugs/insects
—birds
Teacher talk: *What kind of food will the farmers grow?*
What do they need to do to look after their crop?
What do the bugs/insects do on the farm?
What about the birds?

Discuss.
2 Organise children into groups of farmers, bugs and birds and have them discuss their role in the story with their group, then improvise the scene.
3 Back in the class group, discuss the needs of each group for survival (for example air, water, food).
Teacher talk: *What if there were too many bugs eating the plants?*
What would happen to the crops?
What would the farmers do?
How would this affect the bugs?
How would this affect the birds?
4 Have children act out the scene again; this time the farmers spray pesticide to kill the bugs.
5 Discuss the result of this action in terms of air pollution and the eco-system. Ask children to suggest other ways for the farmers to solve the problem which would not pollute the air. Act out the scene again using a different solution. Compare the two.

Air pollution and solutions

Expectations are that children:
- identify ways in which air becomes polluted
- become aware of pollution as a health threat
- recognise the need to change practices which pollute air

○ **Resources:** Open space,
□ candle, matches, glass jar
and lid
△ **Skills:** Questioning,
Inferring, predicting,
observing
Concepts: Fire needs fuel/
oxygen to keep burning,
oxygen levels

1 **Teacher talk:** *Let's pretend we're camping with our families.*
Its getting dark and cold now.
What shall we do to get warm?

Children form family groups, collect wood for a fire and
improvise camp fire scenes.

2 In the class group, discuss what happened to the fuel used in
the fire. Encourage children to comment on the amount of
fuel at the beginning of the fire compared to what might
have been left if the fire had burnt out.
Teacher talk: *Where did the fuel go?*
What kept the fire burning?
Did the fire need things other than wood to keep burning?
Let's see if we can find out!

3 Light a small candle and watch it burn.
Teacher talk: *What is the candle using for fuel?*
Is it using something other than wax to keep it burning?
Could it be the same thing used by the camp fire?

Place the candle in a glass jar and seal it.
Teacher talk: *Why did the fire go out?*
What was inside the jar before I put the candle in?
What do you think the fire did to the air inside the jar?

4 Pass the jar around for children to smell. Ask children how
they would feel if they had to breathe in air like that.

5 Children return to their camp fire scene. Choose a small
group to personify the wind and blow the smoke onto
people sitting around the fire. Encourage children to react
appropriately to the smoke. Discuss. Have children reflect on
wider scale pollution as a result of burning fuels all around
the world.

Resources: Open space, crumpled pieces of newspaper, sheet of paper, textas

Skills: Discussing, describing, identifying, categorising, hypothesising

Concepts: Burning fuels, air pollution, increased carbon dioxide, cause and effect

1 Discuss and list different situations in which fuel is burnt, the kind of fuel used and the purpose for which it is burnt, for example:

—camp fires   to keep warm, to cook—wood
—home fireplaces   to keep warm—wood
—incinerators   to get rid of rubbish—refuse (identify)
—factories   to operate machines—fossil fuels
—barbecues   to cook—wood, 'briquettes' (coal)

2 Children form groups and choose a situation to discuss and then improvise. Walk around to each group, ask focusing questions.
Teacher talk: What are you doing?
What kind of fuel are you using?
Where does it come from?
What is happening to the air around the fire as the fuel burns?

In the class group children share their ideas.

3 Tell the class that the room represents the whole world and they the people in it.
Children crumple up sheets of newspaper to represent different kinds of fuels, for example wood (trees), coal/briquettes, refuse/rubbish, and place around the room.

4 In small groups children improvise a situation from the list, using the fuel (crumpled sheets) around them. Focus children on the task by asking:
Teacher talk: What are you doing? Why?
What kind of fuel are you using?
Most of your fuel is burnt—you'd better get some more!

Continue the improvisation until all the fuel (around the room) has been used.

5 In the class group discuss:
Teacher talk: What happened to the fire when the fuel ran out?
What happened to the air while the fuel was burning?
What will happen if we use up all the trees for fuel?
What will happen to other living things if the air cannot be cleaned?

Draw comparisons between the improvisation and what is actually happening in our environment. Research pollution issues through books, media studies and inviting environmental groups to speak to the class.

○ **Resources:** Open space or outdoor area
Science skills: Inferring, investigating, discovering, observing, predicting, forming conclusions, suggesting
Concepts: Engine—fuel-burning, exhaust emission fumes, air pollution

1 Select an outdoor area to do this activity. Set boundaries to guide children in their use of the area.
   Teacher talk: Let's pretend we're drivers going to work!
   There's a lot of traffic on the road.
   Uh, oh! Watch out for that pedestrian!

   Impress on the children the necessity of obeying traffic rules. Comment on the number of vehicles and the number of people in each during the improvisation. Repeat the improvisation with people coming home from work.
2 Children return to the class group and select first a short then a longer journey—the local shop, a trip to the country.
   Teacher talk: Off you go!
   Don't forget to fill your tank for your trip!

   Children improvise their journeys.
3 In the class group ask individuals about their trips.
   Teacher talk: In which journey did you use the most fuel?
   How many times did you fill your tank?
   What happened to the fuel inside the tank?
   Where did it go?
4 Walk to the school car park. Look at the fuel tank, engine and exhaust pipe of your car.
   Teacher talk: How do you put the petrol in?
   Where does it go inside the car?
   How do you think it is burnt up?
   What comes out of the exhaust pipe?
   Where do the fumes go?

   Encourage children to offer creative suggestions to reduce pollution from fuel emission.

○ ☐ **Resources:** Classroom or open space
Skills: Observing, discussing, hypothesising
Concepts: Air pollution affects breathing, air composition, environmental elements

1 With a partner children show how they would react to the following situations. You are standing too close to:
   —someone smoking a cigarette
   —a barbecue
   —someone using hair spray
   —a car's exhaust pipe
   —an incinerator
   —someone using insecticide
   (Children could add to these suggestions.)
2 Partners in roles present their improvisations to the class group. Others make comments and form conclusions about their observed reactions.
   Teacher talk: Why did they cough/sneeze?
   Was it something in the air they breathed?
   What other living things would be affected by dirty air?
3 Discuss the composition of air and the inter-relatedness of elements in our environment.

Resources: Classroom, textas and poster paper
Skills: Investigating, questioning, forming conclusions, discussing, problem-solving, suggesting
Concepts: Safe work practices, work environments

1 Tell children they are council members of a semi-industrial community at a special meeting to discuss pollution. Their role is to discuss ways to keep the air clean in their city.
2 Children reflect on the problems before coming up with solutions. Take on the role of the minute secretary and scribe suggestions made, for example 'Keep cars out of the city'.
3 Divide the class into two groups, one consisting of the council members and the other made up of different business groups. Ask children to suggest businesses, for example petrol stations, manufacturers, power stations, shops, etc. Have each business group research their role by reading books and looking at pictures of working environments. The council members discuss and list questions to determine if environmentally safe practices are being used by the business groups.
4 When the research period is complete the business groups use classroom furniture to set up their work environment. The council members inspect the work environments and interview business representatives with prepared questions about their work.
5 Have a whole-class sharing session where each group performs their improvisation and the audience reacts with comments and questions about their practices. Use focusing questions to guide the children.
Teacher talk: Can electricity cause pollution? How? Where does electricity come from?

Also reflect on the list of recommendations for clean air compiled earlier.
Teacher talk: Will any of these suggestions help this particular business reduce pollution?
6 Encourage children to reflect on what might happen to life on Earth if air pollution continues.

Using air to make things work
Expectations are that children:
• become aware that air can be used to create energy
• will recognise ways in which air is used

Resources: Open space, pictures of boats/ships (modern and historical)
Skills: Observing, discussing, hypothesising, comparing, recording
Concepts: Wind, air movement, energy, pollution

1 Show the class pictures of sea/water vessels. Discuss what it might be like to travel in them.
With a partner children decide on a vessel to travel in.
Teacher talk: Where will you go? What will you do? What will you need for the journey?

Partners improvise the preparation and their travel.
2 In the class group, children share their boating experiences. Have children select a vessel not powered by a motor and improvise another situation.
Teacher talk: What helps your boat travel (move)? What does it need to get from one place to another?

Compare the speed to a motor-powered vessel.
Teacher talk: Which is faster? Why? Which is less likely to harm our environment? Why?

Resources: Open space, drawing paper, pencils
Skills: Discussing, questioning, inferring, recording, comparing
Concepts: Air movement, energy, wind power, velocity

1 Have children pretend they are people living hundreds of years ago who have decided to find another country to live in far away across the sea.
Teacher talk: How will you get there? How big will the ship be? Will the ship have an engine? Why/why not?
2 Children form groups of families and boat crews, discuss where they are going and what they will need.
3 Members of each group record their decisions by preparing drawings of:
—the clothes they will take with them
—the ship they will sail in
—the food they will need on the journey
—a map that will guide them on their journey
4 With masking tape or chalk outline the shape of the ship on the floor according to the size children think it should be to carry all the people going.
Children improvise the boarding scene.
5 Have children pretend they are in the middle of the ocean with a strong wind blowing.
Teacher talk: Are all the sails up? What is happening to them? How do the sailors help to sail the ship? How is the ship moving? How do the passengers react to the wind?
6 After a while tell the children the wind has stopped blowing.
Teacher talk: The sea is very calm now. What are the sails doing? Do the sailors have them all up? Is the ship moving? How?
7 Back in the class group, children discuss the journey in terms of wind power and the length of the journey compared to modern travel.

Resources: Open space, classroom
Skills: Discussing, questioning, observing, inferring
Concepts: Wind, energy, spatial terms (on top, underneath, around) speed (fast, slow), direction, air movement

1 Ask the class to contribute to a list of things which are powered by air, or in which air is featured, for example: windmill, parachute, vacuum cleaner, hair dryer, kite. Discuss how air is associated with these.
With a partner children become one of the things listed, for example, one child is a hair dryer, the other its user.
2 Partner work is performed to the class. Model focusing questions to encourage the audience to ask their own, for example:
How does it use air?
Where does the air come from?
What does the air do in this situation?
Is it moving fast or slow?
In what direction do you think it is blowing?
How do you know?
3 Discuss air movement in terms of energy to make things work.

Resources: Open space
Skills: Discussing, suggesting, forming conclusions, hypothesising
Concepts: Floating, air lift, spatial terms (outside, around, forward), air mass/weight

1 Tell children to move around the room as if they were floating in air.
Teacher talk: Are you really floating or pretending to?
Have you ever been pushed or lifted by air?
Did you know that air is very powerful?
It can lift me!
It can even lift a bus!
2 *Teacher talk: Let's go on a bus trip!*
Where shall we go?
Are you all ready?
Let's go!

Improvise the bus journey. Encourage comments about what can be seen on the way.
3 After a while, slow down and jerk suddenly to a stop.
Teacher talk: Goodness, what was that awful bang?
I think there's something wrong with the bus.

Have children get off to investigate.
4 Children suggest what the problem might be. If necessary guide them to discover a flat tyre.
Teacher talk: How can we fix it?
What is inside the tyre?
What will we need to pump it up?

Have children reflect on what would happen if all the tyres were flat. Guide children to conclude that air has weight and strength.

Air activities across the curriculum

Language

Write a poem beginning 'Air is all around. . .'

Read the story 'The wind and the sun'; the beginning of *The Wizard of Oz*.

Discuss and write a story about the wind taking you off to another land.

Write verses to promote a pollution-free environment.

Write stories on:
- —I am a fish
- —Trapped in a box

Make a list of words relating to air, for example wind, fly, breeze, drift.

Make a book titled, My book about air; write in it all the things you know about air; illustrate.

Develop slogans about keeping air clean.

Write a group story about living in a heavily polluted city.

Write a story about an air balloon adventure—paste it on a balloon cut-out.

Society

Find out about people living in remote areas of the country—how does erosion affect them?

What are windmills used for?

How important are windmills in Holland?

Who invented the early flying machines? Visit a museum of aviation.

How do people around the world use wind power?

How do people/animals use insulation to keep warm?

How many different ways is air used in people's work?

Find out about people who work underwater.

Set up a display of environmental information at your school.

Environment

How are seed and pollen distributed?

Look for evidence of wind distribution outdoors.

Collect seed pods at different stages of maturity—predict what will happen to the seed if left in the wind; where have seeds from empty pods gone?

How do plants and fish breathe in the sea?
Discuss pictures that show effects of pollution.
Observe the sky—are there signs of pollution?
Why do water plants float in the water. How does the stem differ from land plants?
Outdoors look for signs of damage caused by moisture in the air.
Examine soil from different areas—look for signs of life. Is there enough air in the soil?

Health

List healthy products from the sea which we use in our daily lives.
How do we take in air—what happens to the air inside our bodies?
Invite a nurse to speak on respiratory problems, for example asthma.
Discuss modes of travel—which is of more personal benefit?
Examine foods for evidence of air.
Draw pictures of healthy activities performed outdoors—how important is exercise to good health?

Mathematics

Keep records of daily wind patterns; compile a graph.
Measure the distance you can blow a small crumpled piece of paper through a straw.
Fill a balloon with air; estimate how far it will travel when you release the air? Measure and check your estimate?
Walk outdoors, observe patterns in nature caused by the wind; record them, work out the number pattern.
How can less cars transport more people to their jobs—make a poster of cars illustrating this.
Make a graph showing how each child travels to school—which method is more environmentally safe?
Use balance scales to weigh things containing air.
Does air have weight? Can you find out?

Science

Do balloon experiments:
   —Float a balloon in water, let out the air. What happens?
   —Cut the bottom off a paper cup, make a hole in the centre; pull the balloon's air outlet through the hole, blow it up. Predict what will happen if you put it in water?
Observe birds; do they float, glide or fly in the air?
Make paper shapes that will fly in the air.

Make tiny parachutes from plastic supermarket bags and thread.
Use soapy water and a pipe cleaner to make bubbles.
Use different fuels to keep a fire burning—which make the most smoke/smell?
Observe two identical plants; spray above one with hair spray every day—what changes occur after a period of time?

Art
Make a kite, decorate the tail with different shapes.
Collect bottle tops, odds and ends; make a wind chime by tying onto a coat-hanger.
Make a mobile using an air theme.
Design a windmill; make it out of scrap materials.
Draw air theme designs on balloons; decorate the classroom.
Drop paint spots onto a sheet of paper; blow through a straw to make designs—hold an exhibition of your paintings.
What symbols give helpful messages to people—for example, 'No smoking'?
Design some environmentally friendly symbols.

Music
Invite an airforce band to visit. How do Scottish bagpipes work?
Practise leaf blowing; play a tune.
Listen to an orchestra—identify, name the wind section.
Make a list of wind instruments—how does air help to make music?
Using hollow pipes/straws make a wind instrument; compose a piece of music and perform for other classes.

Technology
Cut pictures of flying machines from magazines, make a poster, label them.
Visit the airport—how many different kinds of machines can you see?
Invite a pilot to visit. Find out about flying machines.
Observe a vacuum cleaner at work. How is the dust deposited inside?
Make a simple air-lifting machine with a balloon.
Visit a maritime museum—what equipment is designed for underwater breathing?

The environment: Section C

Water as a natural resource

Expectations are that children:
- develop an awareness that water covers most of the Earth's surface
- observe weather conditions
- have an understanding of the water cycle

Resources: Notebooks, coloured pencils, globe of the Earth
Skills: Observing, discussing, hypothesising, recording, comparing
Concepts: Planet, Earth, sphere, surface, size, space

1 Children become scientists from another planet sent to observe the Earth from space.
Teacher talk: What planet are you from?
What will you need to record observations?

Scientists take off in their spacecraft. Make comments to help children visualise the journey.

2 As they draw near the Earth focus attention on the Earth's shape, size and colour.
Teacher talk: Look, there's the Earth—the planet with all the blue on it!
What shape is it?
Is it the same shape/size as your planet?
What colours can you see on its surface?

Scientists record the shape of the Earth in their notebooks, using colours they imagine they see from the spacecraft.

3 Scientists compare a globe of the world with their recordings.
Teacher talk: How does your picture compare?
What are all the blue areas?
Is there more land or water on the Earth's surface?

Scientists conclude that Earth has more water than land and turn their spacecraft in the direction of home.

Resources: Open space, poster paper, textas
Skills: Discussing, hypothesising
Concepts: Natural catchment areas

1 ***Teacher talk:*** *Rain collects in puddles, ponds, valleys. In what other places does rain collect?*

Introduce the term 'catchment area'. A small group of children become rain. Other form catchment areas into which rain falls.
Repeat the improvisation with only some rain falling in the catchment areas.
Teacher talk: *Where will the other rain fall? Where does it go when it reaches the ground?*

Children hypothesise and discuss.

Resources: Open space, books on water resources
Skills: Discussing, hypothesising, forming conclusions
Concepts: Evaporation, artesian water, steam, vapour, moisture

1 In pairs children list where they know water to be—indoor or outdoor, for example:
(a) a garden
(b) washing drying on the line
(c) steam coming from a boiling kettle
2 Partners improvise situations from the list.
Children reflect on what happens to water in each situation.
Teacher talk: *What happens to rain in the garden? Where does the water in the washing go? What comes out of the boiling kettle?*

Discuss the feasibility of water in the air and going below the ground surface. Guide children to further resources.

Resources: Outdoor area
Skills: Observing, discussing, identifying, hypothesising
Concepts: Water vapour, weather, clouds

1 Children walk outdoors to find evidence of water and to make observations about the weather.
Teacher talk: *What kind of day is it (wet, windy, cold, sunny)? Do you think it will rain? How do you know?*

Discuss the effect the sun has on water on the ground and other outdoor water.
2 A group of children become the sun—others are puddles in the school-yard.
Teacher talk: *Sunbeams, warm the water! Are you feeling warm, water? What is happening to you? What is happening to the puddle?*
3 Children discuss the improvisation in terms of what occurs when water is heated. Draw children's attention to clouds. Discuss the connection between clouds and the water in the puddle. Introduce the term 'water vapour'.

Resources: Open space
Skills: Presenting, discussing
Concepts: Water vapour, evaporation, clouds, water cycle

1 Groups assume the roles of water and the sun and act out, 'The story of the water cycle'.

Teacher talk: *Water is always moving, in the air, in the lakes, moving in streams and rivers until it reaches the ocean. The sun gently warms the water. Tiny, invisible drops of water vapour float up into the air; up and up they float, until they get cold and huddle together. As they huddle they become clouds. The clouds fill up with more water. They become so heavy that they burst, and fall as drops of rain. The rain falls on the Earth and fills up the lakes, fills up the rivers and fills up the oceans. The sun warms the water, and the story happens all over again.*

Discuss the experience, then repeat the story. Children may wish to present a rehearsed performance to an audience, using coloured fabrics to represent the water, sun and clouds. This would further consolidate children's understanding of the water cycle.

Using water for work and play

Expectations are that children:
• identify ways in which water is used in our community
• become aware of water use in leisure activities

Resources: Open space
Skills: Discussing, suggesting
Concepts: Water use, conservation

1 Discuss water use in the community. Children suggest ways water is used to complete tasks, for example:
—cleaning the car
—watering the garden
—washing clothes
2 Partners mime one of the tasks, then perform it to the class. Encourage the audience to comment on the amount of water used in each task and to suggest ways of using less water.
3 Illustrate our dependence on water by having children try to do the same tasks without water.

Resources: Open space, classroom furniture, equipment, boxes, pictures: water wheels, logging works, hydro-electric power stations, trout farming, transport; books on water industries
Skills: Discussing, hypothesising
Concepts: Precipitation, rivers, gravity, water supply/use

1　Children become raindrops falling on mountains.
　Teacher talk: What will happen to all this rain?
　Will it stay on the mountains?
　Where will it go?

　Briefly discuss the movement of water from high to low levels.
2　Children become a river. Choose leaders to guide the river on the journey to the sea. (Mention the role of precipitation in establishing permanent rivers.)
3　Repeat steps 1 and 2.
　Teacher talk: Look at all this river water—we can't let it go to waste!
　What should we do with it?
　Can we use it in some way?

　Discuss water supply and water use in the community.
4　Show pictures of water use in industry. In small groups children select one of the industries to research. Guide groups to appropriate resources.
5　Groups discuss then improvise an aspect of their research to illustrate how the industry uses water. Encourage children to define their roles and task before the improvisation.
6　Groups research water use in other industries, for example drink factories, mining (oil rigs), fisheries, etc.
　Each group builds an environment using classroom furniture, equipment or cardboard boxes to represent one of these. Groups explain the importance of water in their work.

Resources: Open space
Skills: Discussing, recording, responding
Concepts: States of water: liquid, gas, solid; leisure

1　Discuss and list places that people visit for leisure.
　Partners discuss an activity they would like to do.
　Encourage children to visualise the activity by asking where it will take place, what they will be doing and what will be used.
2　Before improvising children tell the class what their activity will be. Circulate and make focusing comments.
　Teacher talk: That looks like fun!
　You must really enjoy surfing/skiing!
　How often do you go hiking/gliding?
3　Back in the class group, draw children's attention to the list. Discuss whether water is involved in some way in the activities.
4　Partners perform their improvisation to the class. The audience identifies the presence of water in each activity. Guide children by commenting on other forms of water (solid, gas).

Appreciating our water supply

Expectations are that children:
- become aware of the importance of our water supply
- develop a basic understanding of how our water supply works
- develop an appreciation of our water supply

Resources: Open space
Skills: Discussing, hypothesising, decision-making
Concepts: Heritage, needs, water supply/accessibility

1 **Teacher talk:** Let's go on a journey back in time! What do you think the land was like before we came?

Discuss what the land might have looked like.

2 **Teacher talk:** Pretend you are a family who has just arrived to settle on this land.

Organise children into family groups. Have children work out family roles, how they arrived and what they need to do when they get there. Circulate and ask focusing questions.
Teacher talk: Who are the members of your family?
What have you brought with you?
What will you need to stay alive?

3 Allocate a working space to each group where they improvise their arrival and settling in.

4 Children return to the class group in family role and report on their experiences.
Teacher talk: How/where did you get your food?
Where does your water come from?

5 List the different ways families accessed and used their water supply. (Remind children that there is no modern water supply.)
Teacher talk: Where did you find water?
How did you get it to your home?
What was it used for?
What will you do if the supply runs out?

Children hypothesise about the kind of land pioneers preferred to settle on in terms of available resources.

Resources: Open space
Skills: Discussing, hypothesising, problem-solving, valuing
Concepts: Water mains, water sources, hygiene/lifestyle

1 Children form groups of families living in the same street and a group of water maintenance workers. Family groups choose roles and discuss typical household activities involving the use of water. Maintenance workers discuss how they will lay new water pipes in the street.

2 Family groups improvise the family activities. Workers set up their equipment in the street, then approach each household saying that the water will be turned off for the day.

3 Families return to the class group.
*Teacher talk: Will not having water affect your family?
How?
What will you do?
Does your house get water from another source (for example rain tank)?*

Discuss.
4 Families and workers resume their improvisation. Workers carry out their work. Families demonstrate their household routines in the absence of water.
5 In the class group, discuss the implications of having no water in a modern household (for example health, lifestyle). Draw attention to households where running water may not be easily available (for example remote farming communities, small tribal villages around the world). Discuss in terms of appreciation of our present water supply.

Resources: Open space, four placards: 'Reservoir', 'Water treatment plant', 'Holding tank', 'Water main'; household plan of water pipes
Skills: Inferring, hypothesising, discussing, suggesting
Concepts: Water mains, holding tank, reservoir, water treatment

1 *Teacher talk: How may taps inside/outside your house?
Where does the water from your tap come from?
Is it the same place where school tap water comes from?
Let's see if we can find out!*

Walk around the school building. Follow visible pipes leading from taps. Discuss.
2 Show children a plan of water pipes in a suburban house.
*Teacher talk: Where do these pipes lead?
How does the water get into the pipes?*

Children make suggestions.
3 Have children follow water on the journey taking it to their homes. Pairs hold one of the following placards: 'Reservoir', 'Water treatment plant', 'Holding tank', 'Water main'. Groups become residents and water.
4 Tell children to make the sound of falling rain.
*Teacher talk: Look at all this rain!
We can't let it go to waste.
Natural water catchments aren't enough.
Let's save some for our own use.
Into the reservoir the water goes.
Where will it go after that?
Where will it go next?*

The water travels from the 'Reservoir' to the 'Water main'. At the end of the water's journey residents use the water for various household purposes.
5 In the class group discuss the journey. Refer to the household plan showing the end of the journey. Children suggest places supplied by water mains (hospitals, schools, factories) and reflect on the importance of the service.

Water pollution and solutions

Expectations are that children:
- identify some causes of water pollution
- suggest ways pollution can be reduced
- become aware of global pollution

Resources: Open space, sheet of paper, newspaper sheets, textas

Skills: Suggesting, discussing, recording, observing, comparing, defining, planning

Concepts: Pollution

1 *Teacher talk: Our water is becoming more and more polluted.*
How is this happening (oil spills, raw sewage)?
Do we pollute water in any way?

Discuss household practices with cleaning agents, disposal of rubbish and waste products in drains.
Write names of pollutants on the sheet of paper.

2 Each child copies the name of one pollutant onto a sheet of newspaper. Discuss how each pollutant affects water life.

3 Divide the class into groups of people, water plants and sea creatures. Define floor spaces for sea and land. People improvise household activities using water; the others enact underwater scenes.

4 When both groups are well into the improvisation tell the people to begin throwing the pollutants (newspaper sheets) into the sea. Encourage the marine life to react appropriately to the pollutants which are invading their space. People continue to throw the sheets in until none are left.

5 In the class group observe the amount of pollution in the sea and reflect on the activity. Compare it to real-life situations. Make a plan for action against pollution.

Resources: Open space, scrap materials, large painted sign

Skills: Suggesting, discussing, analysing, forming conclusions, decision-making

Concepts: Pollution, causality

1 *Teacher talk: It's holiday time!*
Let's go to our favourite spot up the river.
What shall we do—swim, fish, go boating or waterskiing?

Organise children into groups. Each group discusses and prepares things they will need to take with them. Scrap materials could be used as props for fishing rods, water skis, picnic baskets.

2 *Teacher talk: Are you ready?*
How will you get there?

Children board their transport and set off on a 'long' journey, outdoors, around school buildings and back into the classroom which becomes their destination.

3 Make comments to help children visualise the environment. Children find a spot to set up things and begin to explore the environment.

4 Suddenly draw attention to a sign you have discovered. (The sign was prepared before the lesson without the children's knowledge.)
Teacher talk: *Stop everyone, look!*
Come and have a look at this.

Read the sign with the children.

5 Discuss the implications of the sign. Have children make conclusions about how the water might have become polluted.

Water activities across the curriculum

Language
Make a set of class books showing water use for leisure, home/school.
Write stories about:
  • Sunken treasure
  • Lost at sea
  • Living on a houseboat
  • I am a mermaid.
Write daily weather reports; present them during morning talks.
Read stories/poems about rivers/sea.
Write words describing water on rain-drop shapes, suspend from the ceiling.
Do a storyboard: the life of a raindrop.
Read Aesop's fable, 'The raven and the pitcher'.
Make up water poems.

Mathematics

Time how long it takes ice to melt. How long does ice take to melt in three different places?

Collect data about daily weather—make a graph to show patterns over a week.

Fill identical containers with the same amount of water, place an object in each—measure again, compare.

Find five things that hold liquid; estimate how much each holds.

Compare liquid measure of bottles.

How is ice-cream measured: by weight or liquid measure? Why?

Fill clear plastic containers with water to different levels, estimate the height of each level, measure.

Society

Research water travel.

Draw a plan of a house showing water pipes.

Illustrate how people got water supplies in pioneer days.

Draw a collection of clothing for wet weather.

Research water birds; visit the river/sea to observe them.

Research water animals; sort into domestic, wild and pets.

Research rice-growing countries.

Make a poster of foods that need water to cook in.

Science

Place a balloon over the neck of a bottle; place it in hot water—what happens? Why?

Tie a plastic bag over a shoot of a pot plant—what happens in an hour?

Hold a lid over boiling water—what happens underneath the lid?

Fill a dry glass jar with ice—what happens to the outside of the jar?

Collect water from the sea, tap and river—what changes occur in time?

Observe what happens to salt, paper, oil, and sponges in water.

Fill a glass with water, leave for an hour—what are the bubbles?

Place objects in water—which float/sink? Predict, then record.

Environment

On a poster illustrate how sun, air, soil, water interact.

Visit a mangrove; observe trees, plants in water. How do they take in air?

Make a miniature mountain; use a watering can for rain; make a river.

Walk outdoors after rain; observe areas with and without puddles—why does water collect in some and not others?

Make a list of hints for saving water. Look for signs of pollution in/near water—what caused it?

Visit the local government office—enquire about pollution prevention.

Is water a renewable energy source?

Art

Paint a design with water colours; splash water on with fingertips.

On cloud shapes, draw water scenes; suspend from ceiling.

Paint a sea scene, use three strands of colour; press wet sponges on it.

Experiment with marbling designs using oil paints and water.

Music

Listen to Handel's Water Music.

Make up songs about water.

Collect songs about rain/water, sing them at a 'Water show'.

Make music by blowing across openings of bottles—do they sound different when partly filled with water?

Fill glasses with different amounts of water; 'play' them with spoons.

Tape a symphony of water sounds, for example dripping tap, rain, splashing, etc.

Health

Have someone trace around your body; colour to a level to illustrate how much water your body holds.

How much fluid intake do we need? Do we require more in some instances? Draw to illustrate.

Bring in fruit from home—which has the most water?

Illustrate with pictures/drawings how water pollution affects animals.

Discuss hygiene—draw pictures showing how water keeps us healthy.

Collect labels of fruit juice used by your family; read the labels; how much water is mixed with the juice?

Find out about water therapy. How do handicapped/sick people use it?

Technology
Make model water-wheels with paper cups and scrap materials.
Make unusual water-using machines, for example a bug/insect shower.
Make machines powered by water out of scrap materials.
Design/make bridges for waterways.
Make a water mains system using cardboard cylinders.
Design/make water-powered machines with scrap materials.
Make out of plasticine water vessels which float.

Society/Social Studies

Society/Social Studies

Ourselves—being and doing

Expectations are that children:

- identify common actions performed by people
- become aware of differences in abilities
- understand that people have feelings

Resources: Open space
Skills: Discussing, comparing, forming conclusions
Concepts: Body parts, physical similarities/differences

(a)

1 In their personal space children become string puppets. Call out body parts. Children move the part of the body named.
2 Organise the class into pairs. One child becomes a puppet, the other calls out simple actions, for example, 'Clap your hands', 'Nod your head'.
  Partners swap roles and repeat the activity.
3 In the class discuss actions performed by a single body part.
  Teacher talk: *What did you do with your hand?*
  What else can you do with your hand?
  Can everyone do that? Let's try!

Children perform different actions for each body part and make conclusions about physical similarities which enable people to perform common actions.

Activities (a) and (b) have a follow-through theme and can be taught in sequence or alone.

Resources: Open space
Skills: Inferring, responding, forming conclusions
Concepts: Body parts, physical abilities disabilities

(b)

1 Call out actions with some degree of difficulty. In role of string puppets children perform them.
  Teacher talk: *Rub your tummy with your left hand and tap your head with the other.*
  Do a cartwheel.
2 Organise children into pairs. One becomes the puppet and the other calls the actions.
3 Individuals demonstrate to the class.
4 List some of the tasks performed and the body part(s) involved.
  Teacher talk: *What body parts did you use to turn a cartwheel?*
  Can we all do cartwheels? Why not?
  Who can stand on their head? Why not?

Guide children to conclude that physical similarities do not determine what people can do.
5 Have children reflect on physical disabilities.
  Teacher talk: *How would you write if you had only one hand? How would you find your way around if you could not see?*

Have children perform tasks with one hand behind their backs or wearing blindfolds.

Resources: Open space
Skills: Describing, defining, observing, analysing
Concepts: Feelings/ emotions, facial expression

1 Children pretend they are watching television with a friend. Partners decide beforehand whether their program will be funny, exciting, scary and so on. Comment to encourage appropriate reactions to the program.
Teacher talk: That must be a very funny program!
Why are you so sad—what's happening?
2 Divide the class into two groups. One group become the television viewers, the other observers. The observers' job is to look at the viewers' faces to determine the feelings the program elicits. Allocate an observer to each viewer.
3 Observers share their observations and viewers confirm their accuracy.
Teacher talk: What do you think Tony was feeling?
How do you know?
What were some feelings shown on people's faces?
Did all the viewers have feelings?
How do you know?

Resources: Open space
Skills: Identifying, defining, making conclusions
Concepts: Feelings/ emotions, body language

1 Children choose a partner. Number each pair 1 and 2. Number 1 demonstrates a feeling with an appropriate action. Number 2 mirrors the action.
Partners exhibit various feelings in this way and take turns in leading and reflecting the action.
2 Partners present their work to the class. The audience attempt to identify feelings exhibited. Encourage children to give reasons for their choices.
Conclude that feelings are exclusive to human beings.

Resources: Open space, paper and pencils
Skills: Discussing, presenting, comparing
Concepts: Physical characteristics, ability/ talent, differences and similarities

1 Have children pretend they are artists sketching the portrait of a famous person. Choose a child to become the model. Discuss the characteristics of the subject before beginning.
2 Children use real materials to do the sketch. Children display their completed work.
Teacher talk: Are there any drawings which are exactly the same?
There are differences in your drawings even though you were drawing the same person? Why?

Discuss in terms of abilities and talents.
3 The artists hang their work in an 'art gallery'.
Assuming the role of visitors to the gallery they comment on and make comparisons about the sketches.

○ **Resources:** Open space
□ **Skills:** Discussing,
△ analysing, comparing,
problem-solving
Concepts: Feelings/
emotions, differences in
behaviour

1 Ask children to think of a situation in which people may show strong feelings, for example:
—being lost
—stuck in a lift
—caught in a fire
Choose one situation for all groups to discuss, then improvise to show their feelings in the situation.
2 Each group performs their improvisation to the class.
Teacher talk: What did the people in group one do?
What did group two do in the same situation?
Did they all have the same feelings?
3 Groups repeat the improvisation with the view of solving the problem faced in the situation. Children perform the new improvisation to the class.
Teacher talk: How did group two solve the problem?
Did all the groups solve the problem in the same way? Why not?

Conclude that people do not do things in the same way.

Communicating—feelings and body language

Expectations are that children:
• understand that body language communicates meaning
• identify emotions communicated by body language
• become aware of indicators which give information about a person

---

○ **Resources:** Open space
□ **Skills:** Discussing,
hypothesising,
responding, comparing
Concepts: Feelings/
emotions, human thought

1 Children move around the room as robots. Suggest tasks they could do.
2 Organise partners—one is the robot and the other the operator. The operator tells the robot to perform several tasks. Partners swap roles and repeat the activity.
3 In the class group discuss how the robot works.
Teacher talk: Who decides how it will move and what it will do?
What would happen if no instructions were given?
4 Partners repeat the above activity. The operators add some complexity to the task or give an instruction the doer may be reluctant/unable to complete (that is standing on your head or climbing up the wall).
Partners swap roles and repeat the activity.
5 Children return to the class group.
Teacher talk: Did you do everything asked of you? Why/Why not?

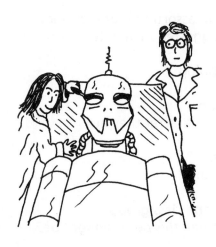

How did you feel when completing the task?
Which role did you prefer (instructor or robot)?

Invite a child to become the doer. Class members ask the child to perform tasks. Have children reflect on how the child responded/reacted to each instruction.
Teacher talk: *Could Jenna do all she was asked?*
What did she do when she didn't understand the task?
How do you think Jenna felt when asked to stand on her head?
How was her behaviour different to the robot?

Make comparisons between robot activity and human activity.
Discuss people's ability to think and feel.

Resources: Open space
Skills: Identifying, observing, discussing
Concepts: Feelings affect body language

1 Have children walk around the room in an anti-clockwise direction. Use the freeze signal to have children change direction. Do this several times.
2 Children return to the class group and sit in a circle.
Teacher talk: *Did you think about what you were doing as you walked?*
Would the way you feel change the way you walk?

Discuss.
3 Invite children to share something which has happened to them and to identify a feeling in that situation, for example:
'My football team won. I felt happy.'
'I lost my pet cat. I felt sad.'
'Someone broke my new toy. I felt angry.'
List some of the events.
4 Each child selects a situation and feeling they identify with and show how they walk when experiencing the feeling. Make comments to individuals as they walk.
Teacher talk: *You look very excited about something?*
Why are you so sad?
5 Individuals show their walk to the class. The audience attempt to identify the feeling behind the walk.

Resources: Open space
Skills: Discussing, reflecting, identifying, hypothesising, forming conclusions
Concepts: Feelings/ emotions, body posture, facial expression, appearance, movement

1 Children cut out pictures of people from magazines and make a poster collage. Discuss people's appearance and reflect on what this tells us about a person.
Teacher talk: *What is the person wearing?*
How is it being worn?
Does this tell you anything about the person?
What feelings do you see in the facial expression?
2 Children become the character in a picture and present it in tableau form. Comment on body posture and facial expression.

3 Each child selects an item from an assortment of costumes and props and assumes a role suggested by the item, for example:
—handbag—woman going shopping
—straw hat—person sunbaking
—briefcase—businesswoman/man
Children assume the walk of the character they are portraying.
Circulate asking focus questions.
Teacher talk: Where are you going?
What will you do there?

4 Individuals perform their role in the class group.
Teacher talk: How old do you think this person might be?
What is the person wearing?
How is the scarf/hat being worn?
How much do we know about the person by the way they look/move?

Discuss how body language, appearance and how a person walks can give information about that person.

Living with others—the family

Expectations are that children:
- identify family relationships and roles
- Identify ways they relate to relatives, friends, neighbours
- become aware of differences and similarities between families

Resources: Open space
Skills: Discussing, identifying, comparing
Concepts: Family roles, family composition

(a)

1 *Teacher talk: What happens at your house at dinner-time?*
Who makes the dinner?
How many people eat the dinner?
Who are they?

Discuss.

2 Organise children into family groups. Group members assume family roles and improvise what happens at one of the group member's homes at dinner-time.

3 Children perform the improvisation to the class. Class members try to identify the people in the family and their roles.
Teacher talk: Who are the members of this family?
What did the father/mother do?
What did the children do?

Activities (a) and (b) have a follow-through theme and can be taught in sequence or alone.

○ **Resources:** Open space
□ **Skills:** Discussing, defining, comparing, hypothesising
Concepts: Family, role differences/similarities, role reversal

Record responses on a large sheet of paper. Have the class make comparisons between families in terms of family composition and roles portrayed.

(b)
1 *Teacher talk: What jobs need doing at your house? Who usually does them?*

Discuss.
Organise children into groups of families. Groups identify roles and tasks performed by each.
2 Choose two groups to perform their improvisation to the class. Make comparisons between the two.
Teacher talk: What were some things that were the same/different in both families?
Who did the washing, ironing, cleaning, etc.?
3 *Teacher talk: What would happen if people in the same family swap jobs?*
Let's see!

Groups repeat the improvisation with family members swapping tasks. For example, if mother has done the cooking then father will next.
4 Children perform their improvisations to the class. Ask whether it matters who does particular tasks.

○ **Resources:** Open space
Skills: Responding, forming conclusions
Concepts: Interaction with others

1 *Teacher talk: What things do you like doing?*

Record responses. Children mime from the activities listed.
2 Circulate and ask focusing questions.
Teacher talk: You said you liked playing in the park.
Who do you play with?
You like gardening don't you—who do you garden with?
3 Have children say who they do things with, for example friends, family members, neighbours or relatives. Children improvise activities they do with different people.
Teacher talk: What things do you do mostly with your family?
What things do you do with others?

Have children conclude that they do different things with different people.

○ **Resources:** Open space
Skills: Suggesting, reporting, discussing
Concepts: Interacting with others, relationships

1 *Teacher talk: It's Sunday—your family is going visiting! Who will you visit?*

Children make suggestions.

2 In groups of four, children organise themselves into visitors and people doing the visiting.
Teacher talk: Get yourselves ready—it's time to go!

Children knock on the door of the person(s) they are visiting and improvise the situation.

3 Children return to the class group, say who they visited and what their relationship is to that person. List on a sheet of paper.

4 Divide the class into groups who visited friends, relatives or neighbours. Each group discusses their relationship with the people they visited. Circulate asking focusing questions.
Teacher talk: What do you do with that person?
How do you feel about that person?
Do you like them? How much?

Groups convey what they understand about the relationships discussed to the whole class.

Our community—differences and similarities

Expectations are that children:
• become aware of differences and similarities within their community
• identify the needs of a community
• understand that communities are groups of people living/working together in the same environment

Resources: Classroom equipment and furniture
Skills: Describing, inferring, forming conclusions
Concepts: Community—environment/composition

1 Ask children to describe their community.
Teacher talk: The school is in our community.
Is it in the city or country?
What's in the same street?
What's in the next street?
Who lives there?
Are there any shops/businesses?

2 Children become workers and build a new housing estate using desks, chairs and classroom equipment.
Teacher talk: Where will the street be?
Are there houses on both sides of the street?
Are there any parks?
Where will you put the shops?

3 When the environment is completed ask children what was built and if anything else needs to be added.
Teacher talk: I can see houses, shops, parks, etc.
Is it a community?
What else does it need (people)?

4 Children form groups of four or five and become families. Each group takes turns to move into the new environment.
Teacher talk: Would it still be a community if no people were living in it? Why/Why not?

Resources: Open space
Skills: Responding, defining, suggesting
Concepts: Community groups/roles

1 Children describe the people who live in their community.
Teacher talk: Are they young/middle-aged/old?
Where do they live?
What do they do?
Do they go out to work or stay at home?
What kind of work do they do?
2 Individuals assume the role of someone they know in their community, (shop owner, petrol station attendant, postal delivery officer).
3 Children perform their role to the class. List each community member portrayed on paper.
Teacher talk: Who else is part of your community?
Who delivers the paper/milk?

Add to children's suggestions.
4 Children assume another role from the list. Before portraying the character children say who they are and what age group they are in.
5 Children draw a picture of their character and paste on a poster titled 'People in our community'. Have children discuss the differences and similarities between people in the community.

Resources: Open space
Skills: Discussing, suggesting, observing
Concepts: Location, environment, groups, needs, goods/services

1 *Teacher talk: Let's make up our very own community!*
Where will our community be (seaside, hills, city, country)?
What shall we call it?
Who will live/work there?

Discuss and write up children's suggestions.
2 A small group of children assume a role from the list. In role they say who they are and what they do. (Ensure that there is a balance of goods/services and family representatives.)
Teacher talk: A community is a group of people.
The group of people is made up of smaller groups.
Let's make up some small community groups!
3 Each community representative selects one or two class members to form a group with, for example:
—real estate agent—'I need a secretary to work in my business.'
—supermarket manager—'I need some shop assistants.'
—clothes shop manager—'I need two sales assistants.'
—parent—'I look after my family—I have one child and a husband.'

4 Two family groups improvise moving into their new neighbourhood while others observe.
Teacher talk: Families have just moved into the community. What will they need to live there (clothes, food, services)?

5 Business/service groups move into the community and set up in response to family needs.

6 Groups improvise living/working in the community.

7 In the class group have children reflect on the needs and roles of different people portrayed. Impress upon the children the difference between needs and wants.
Teacher talk: What did all the people need (food, clothing, shelter)?
What things do some people need and not others (schools, senior citizen homes)?

Animals and people

Expectations are that children:

- differentiate between pets and domestic animals
- become aware of their responsibility toward animals
- identify animals that are important to their lives

Resources: Open space
Skills: Responding, forming conclusions
Concepts: Caring, responsibility, interaction, needs

1 *Teacher talk: What's a pet?*
What can you do with a pet?

With a partner children take on roles of pet and owner and demonstrate.
Teacher talk: Who owns a pet: What is it?
If you don't have one what kind would you like to have?

Make a list of pets.

2 Partners mime the pet's feeding time.
3 Ask children what they do to look after their pet apart from feeding it.
   Teacher talk: *Do all pets need the same care? Why/why not?*

   Children mime another action which shows them caring for their pet, for example:
   —brushing a long-hair cat
   —trimming a dog's fur
   —walking a dog
4 ***Teacher talk:*** *Is it important for your pet to be patted/ridden/taken for walks, etc.?*

   Children pretend they are the pet that is cold, hungry, thirsty or lonely. Have children reflect on the pet's behaviour in each instance.

Resources: Open space
Skills: Identifying, reporting, hypothesising, forming conclusions
Concepts: Living things, animals—domestic/wild, causality/change, responsibility

1 Tell children that they share the world with lots of living things—ask them to name some.
   Teacher talk: *Can you imagine a world of animals but no people?*
2 The class goes on a journey to the land of animals. Children close their eyes and pretend they are on a magic carpet. Talk the children through their journey.
   Teacher talk: *Can you feel the carpet lift?*
   Gently, gently up in the air we go.
   Feel the wind in your faces.
   Hold on tight, we're just about to land!
   Down, down we go.
3 On arrival tell children to be very quiet so that the animals won't be afraid.
   Teacher talk: *You need to be a very gentle and caring person before you are able to see them.*

   Tiptoe around with the children and whisper from time to time and ask what they see.
4 Call children back to the magic carpet and return home. At the end of the journey children share their experiences. Ask focusing questions to help them form conclusions.
   Teacher talk: *Did the animals look comfortable in their environment?*
   What would happen if we took them away from their homes?
   Where did our animals come from before they were pets/domestic animals?
   Who changed the lives of animals?
   Who is now responsible for our pets/domestic animals?

○ **Resources:** Open space/classroom
Skills: Categorising, discussing
Concepts: Animals—domestic/wild/pets

1 The class makes a list of animals which includes pets, domestic and wild. Write each on a card. Write 'domestic', 'wild', and 'pets' on larger cards and place them in three different places in the room.
2 One child at a time picks an animal and mimes it. The class puts the animal in the place where they think it belongs.
3 When all animals have been mimed and categorised discuss the placement of the animals and whether they have been placed in the appropriate category.

People around the world

Expectations are that children:
• become aware that they are part of a larger world community
• understand the common needs of people around the world
• become aware of similarities and differences between people from other countries

○ ☐ **Resources:** World globe, map of own country, maps of various countries, string, streamers
Skills: Discussing, comparing, hypothesising, questioning, researching
Concepts: Country, world, people—differences/similarities, language

1 Discuss characteristics of the world globe.
What are all the blue patches?
What are the other shapes?
What shape is our country?
Can you find it?
2 Look at a map of your own country. Discuss its characteristics. Choose a small group of children to organise class members into a rough outline of the country.
3 *Teacher talk: You are now a country!*
Have you got water around you?
Is there another country next to you?
Who lives in you?
Who lives in the country next door?

Discuss.
4 In the class group, draw children's attention to the globe. Point to and name different countries.
Teacher talk: Do these people speak the same language?
Do they dress the same?
Do they do the same things?
Let's find out.

Organise children into groups according to the country they wish to study. Ask each group to write lists of questions they want answered and begin research from an assortment of resource materials provided.

○
□ **Resources:** Open space, map of own country
Skills: Observing, identifying, researching, forming conclusions
Concepts: Lifestyles around the world, cultural differences/similarities

1 Group children according to a country they are researching. With string (use a map as a guide) children make a large shape of the country on the floor.
2 Children imagine they are a family living in that country and improvise a domestic scene inside the shape of the country (for example a family meal).
(Before the improvisation have children work out who they are and their family roles.)
3 Children perform their group work to the class. Question children to help determine the authenticity of their scene.
Teacher talk: What did the people eat?
Where was the food eaten?
What kind of work did mother/father do?
What did the children do?
Do we do the same things in our country?
4 The class identifies similarities and differences between people from different countries in the given circumstances. Ask children to identify one or more things that all have in common, that is families.
5 Refer children to more resources to check on any inaccuracies evident in the improvisation.

○
□ **Resources:** Open space
Skills: Responding, hypothesising, discussing
Concepts: Cultural differences/similarities (languages)

1 Do we all look the same?
Do we all dress the same?
Can we speak the same language?
What would happen if we all spoke a different language?

Children walk around the room in a clockwise direction. On the freeze signal children stop and greet the person closest to them in nonsense language, for example:
'Globbi moddi'—good morning.
Do this a few times with children adding simple statements and questions, for example:
Hoo dee joo?—How are you?
2 Organise children into pairs. One person tells the partner to perform a simple task in nonsense language, for example 'Walk to the corner' or 'Jump ten times'.
3 Discuss the difficulty of not understanding different languages.

○
□
△ **Resources:** Open space
Skills: Discussing, responding, describing
Concepts: Cultural differences/similarities, needs—shelter, food, warmth

1 *Teacher talk: People from other countries often speak languages we cannot understand.*
What other differences are there between people?

Discuss briefly.

2 Show pictures of people's homes around the world. Discuss.
Teacher talk: *Pretend you live in another country.*
You have to build a home for your family.
What country are you from?
Where will you build your home (environment)?
What will it be made of?
How many people will live in it?

With a partner children improvise the task.

3 Partners describe the home they have built. Have children reflect on the common needs of people around the world (shelter, food, warmth).

Society/Social Studies activities across the curriculum

Language
Write stories about animals; put them in animal-shaped books.
Write letters to:
 —the witch of Purpleland
 —your smelly sneakers
 —the tree in your backyard
 —your relatives.
Draw a robot; write instructions to operate it.
Pick a name out of the telephone book—make up a description of the person.
Make up rhymes titled, 'People in the neighbourhood'.
Write a shopping list of favourite foods.
Write a book on, 'Me and my family'—have a book launch, invite your family.

Mathematics
Make a street picture using pentagons/squares; number the houses.
Walk down your street, count house numbers—where are the higher/lower numbers?
Draw symmetrical pictures of vegetable/fruit families.
Estimate and measure height of teachers in the school.
List jobs you/parents do in a week; record how long it takes to do each.
Make graphs of eyes/hair colour differences in the class.
Measure height of children in the class; compare.

Society

Set up a photo exhibition of family celebrations.
Cut pictures of community events out of the local paper.
Make a map of an imaginary land, name it, mark out rivers, cities, mountains. Decide who lives there and what language is spoken.
Invite relatives in to speak of their cultural backgrounds.
Have a grandparents afternoon tea.
Draw a wardrobe for travelling to:
   —a very cold climate
   —a hot humid climate, etc.
Look at the 'Employment section' of the newspaper—label into goods/service occupations.

Science

Find out about hatching eggs. Observe changes in eggs caused by heat.
Collect plant cuttings; pot for someone special in the community.
Observe animals in the classroom (mice/chicks); record characteristics.
Define characteristics of animals into 'feather, fur or fin'.
Report and record habits of pets.

Environment

Plan a family picnic—what are people's responsibilities if using a natural environment?
Make a 3-dimensional map of your local neighbourhood.
Find out what kind of animals live in your country—which ones have become extinct? Are any others threatened with extinction?
Walk around your community; record all animals seen; organise data into a chart.

Art

Draw/paint portraits of a family of fruit/vegetable monsters.
Paint 'feeling' pictures, for example an angry/happy picture.
Draw 'photos' of yourself at different ages:
   baby, now, teenager, adult, older.
Make an animal shape collage.
Make animal shapes on paper with string and glue.

Music

List favourite animal songs; sing them at assembly.
Interview teachers/parents on their musical tastes; listen to their music—what do you prefer?
Listen to 'The Carnival of the Animals' by Saint-Saëns.

Health

Design/write 'thank-you' notes to your parents for caring for you.

Taste a range of foods blindfolded; say what you are eating.

Write/illustrate:

   'I feel happy when. . .'

List food likes/dislikes in your family; compare with other families.

List all products used by your family before/during breakfast.

Bring to school empty food cartons used by your family—list the natural ingredients.

Make a class book of likes/dislikes.

Technology

Design/invent new re-cyclable product packaging.

Make a robot of scrap materials.

Pull apart old clocks/electrical appliances and examine.

Draw machines to help disabled people.

With scrap materials make machines to weigh/measure:

   —elephants

   —hippopotami

   —giraffes, etc.

Science and energy

Science and energy: Section A

Exploring energy

Expectations are that children:
- develop an understanding of energy
- become aware that life on Earth depends on energy
- recognise the sun as an unique source of energy

Resources: Classroom, magazines, scissors, paste
Skills: Investigating, hypothesising, inferring, questioning, forming conclusions
Concepts: Energy sources

1 Divide the class into groups of four. One child in each group is an inventor, the others are machine parts for assembling. Groups decide what kind of machine and its purpose.
2 The inventors begin their machines. Tell them to work quickly because the supervisor will arrive soon to test the machines.
3 In role of supervisor, circulate, asking questions about the machines' function. The supervisor attempts to start the machines without success. Inventors come up with suggestions as to why the machines will not operate.
4 The supervisor calls a meeting of the 'board of inventors'. (The 'machines' can asssume the role of inventors for this.) Ask the inventors to name different machines—ask what each needs in order to operate.
5 The inventors build their machines again—this time an energy source is added.
6 The inspector inspects and starts the machines. Children conclude that machines can only operate with an energy source.

Resources: Open space (outdoor/indoor)
Skills: Hypothesising, inferring
Concepts: Energy, power source, kilojoules

1 *Teacher talk: Pretend you are a famous tennis player. You need to warm up before your big match.*
People are cheering. You're feeling fit and full of energy.

In pairs children perform the warm-up.
2 In role of interviewer talk to players about their fitness.
Teacher talk: How fit are you?
How have you been training for the match (exercise, food, rest)?
3 Partners act out the tennis match. After the match interview individuals in front of the class group.
Teacher talk: Are you feeling tired after your match?
When did you have the most energy, now or before the match? Why?
Can you build up your energy again? How?
Children discuss the purpose of food, drink, exercise and rest.
4 Children take role of other athletes or workers. The class can be divided into athletes/workers and journalists.

Resources: Open space
Skills: Discussing, hypothesising, observing, comparing
Concepts: Energy levels, movement energy, eco-system, growth

1 Brainstorm things that can move (for example machines, skates, boats, playground swings) and list.
Children mime one thing from the list.
Use the freeze signal to have children mime something else from the list. Repeat this until several things are mimed.
Teacher talk: Who's feeling hot?
How did your body get hot?
Can your body keep going all the time? Why not?
2 Choose individuals to repeat their mime while others observe.
Teacher talk: Does this thing move all the time? Why/Why not?
When does it stop?
What will it need to keep moving?
3 Have children mime an activity with high energy consumption (running) and one with low energy (walking).
Teacher talk: When do you think you need the least energy?
Is there any time when your body does not need energy?

Discuss the importance of energy for growth.
Discuss movement energy and compare energy sources of living/non-living things.

Resources: Open space
Skills: Discussing, inferring, identifying, questioning, hypothesising
Concepts: Sun as an energy source, transference of energy, eco-system

1 *Teacher talk: Where does energy come from?*
Where do plants get their energy to grow?
Where do machines get their energy to work?

Make a list of living and people-made things which move.
Children mime to show how energy is used in each.
2 Invite children to present a mime to the class. The audience identifies what is being presented and asks questions relating to its energy source. Model follow-through questions to guide children, for example:
A horse—Where does your energy come from? (food)
Where does hay come from?
Where do plants come from?
What helps the plant to grow?

A car—What helps you go? (fuel)
Where does petrol/oil come from?
How did it get into the ground?
What was it before it became oil?

Discuss the transference of energy from the sun, draw diagrams to illustrate. Have children imagine what would happen without the sun's energy.

Sources of energy

Expectations are that children:
- identify sources of energy
- understand how some energy sources are used

○ **Resources:** Open space, note-pad, pencils
Skills: Discussing, observing, recording, investigating
Concepts: Energy sources (fuels, electricity, wind, etc.)

1 Children find their personal space. Call out several different actions for children to perform (hop, jump, skip) until children have warmed up.
Teacher talk: Are you feeling warm?
You've used quite a bit of body energy doing those things!
What other things in our school use up energy?

2 Children become detectives and go on an 'energy hunt' and record evidence of energy use (other than body energy). Children bring a real note-pad and pencil.
With partners children go outdoors and observe things moving, for example:
—a flag flying
—leaves moving
—cars
—birds
—water sprinklers
Indoors observe:
—lights
—clocks
—computers
—telephones, etc.

3 In the classroom children share their observations.
Teacher talk: What did you see?
How was energy involved?
How many kinds of energy did you see?
Which energy source was being used the most?

○ □ **Resources:** Open space, sheet of paper
Skills: Describing, problem-solving, discussing
Concepts: Sources of energy, energy consumption

1 Children become family groups returning home from camping.
Teacher talk: You've just walked in the front door.
It is night-time.
You are tired, hungry and dirty.
What will you do first?

Allocate a working space for each group. Children improvise the situation. Circulate and comment on their activities.

2 Children return to the class group and say what they did to meet their needs. Ask children how these needs were met on camp. Record on a sheet of paper, for example:

It was dark/cold—what did you do about it?

Camp	Home
Used a torch	Switched on the light
Lit a fire	Turned on the heater

3 Some groups improvise how they solved the problem of cold, cleanliness/darkness on camp while others solve the same problems in the home setting.
4 Discuss the sources of energy used in different settings to fulfil the same needs.

Resources: Open space/classroom, scrap materials, scissors, glue, stapler, masking tape
Skills: Discussing, hypothesising, designing, creating
Concepts: Wind power, solar heating, alternative energy sources, energy conservation, renewable energy

1 Children pretend they are sailing or wind-surfing.
Teacher talk: What kind of energy is helping you move?

Discuss wind power as being environmentally safe and renewable.
2 *Teacher talk: You are in an empty house.*
It's just being built and the power is not yet connected.
It is the middle of the day in winter.
Find the warmest part of the house to stand in?

Children say what spot they chose and why they think it was the warmest. Ask children what energy source was keeping them warm.
3 Tell children to trap the sun's warmth and use it to heat the other parts of the house. With partners children discuss and make an 'energy storer' out of scrap materials.
4 Partners place the completed receptacles in the warmest part of the house. Children discuss ways in which the stored energy could be used.

Energy conservation

Expectations are that children:
• become aware of non-renewable energy sources
• perceive the need for energy conservation
• identify ways energy can be saved

Resources: Open space
Skills: Discussing, comparing, inferring, hypothesising, problem-solving
Concepts: Heat, cold, energy efficiency/economy, solar energy

1 Children discuss activities they do on warm sunny days and wet cold days and make comparisons.
Teacher talk: What do you like doing best?
What weather do you prefer? Why?
2 Divide the class in half—one group improvises sunny weather activities and the other cold weather activities.

3 In the class group share experiences.
Teacher talk: Were you warm or cold?
What did you do to keep warm?
What keeps you warm on sunny days?
Which is the cheapest way to keep warm?

4 Discuss indoor heating. Have children say what fuels are used in their homes for heating.
Teacher talk: What do you do if you run out of oil/gas/coal?
If all the fuel in the world was used up how would you keep warm?

5 Organise children into groups of scientists. Tell them that fuels are running out and they need to find some other ways of solving indoor heating. Remind children that the sun is a unique source of heat. Groups discuss and improvise solutions.

6 In the class group, scientists perform solutions found. Guide children to appropriate resources on solar energy.

Resources: Open space, household appliance catalogues, scissors, glue, cardboard
Skills: Categorising, problem-solving, discussing, hypothesising, forming conclusions
Concepts: Energy conservation, renewable/non-renewable energy sources

1 Children cut pictures from electrical appliance catalogues and paste on cards.

2 Group children into families, select a floor space for their house and furnish it with the electrical appliances (cards). Family members then use the appliances.

3 When the improvisation is well in progress introduce a power failure. In the class group, children discuss power failures from their own experiences.
Teacher talk: What happened when the lights went out?
How did your family solve the problem?

4 Children continue the improvisation from the point where the power stopped and demonstrate how they solve the problem.

5 In the class group, discuss what would happen if the power never returned. Make a list of energy sources and categorise into renewable and non-renewable (wood, fossil fuels). Guide children to more information from books, charts, environmental videos, etc.

Resources: Pictures of households using energy
Skills: Discussing, recording, hypothesising
Concepts: Energy conservation, alternative energy sources

1 Show pictures of people using energy in their homes, for example:
  (a) the bathroom—using an electric shaver
  (b) the laundry—putting clothes in the dryer
  (c) the kitchen—cutting food with an electric knife
Groups make a tableau of each situation. On a given signal the tableaux come to life, on the freeze signal they become still. Use the two signals to provide contrast of stillness/movement.

2 Groups perform the same situation again but demonstrate practices which reduce energy consumption.
Teacher talk: What can dry clothes instead of a dryer? What can be used instead of an electric knife?
3 Children discuss and list ways energy can be saved in their own homes.

Energy activities across the curriculum

Language
Brainstorm words relating to energy sources—use webbing to illustrate.
Read/write stories about pioneers.
Write 'if' stories:
   'If the world had no electricity/motor transport'
Make a class book showing how energy is used in the school.
Write an advertisement for an energy-saving household appliance.
Use each letter in the word 'energy' to begin a word to describe its meaning.
Write an imaginary recipe for 'energy soup'.
Make paper flags; write things which use wind energy on each.

Mathematics
Collect data of motor vehicles driving past the school—compile a graph, show the number and kind of vehicles.
Which room in the school/home uses the most electricity? Make a graph of usage.
Time high/low energy tasks, compare.
Look at the lesson timetable; label each high/low energy; estimate time spent on each category in a week.
Estimate/measure speed of cars/people/animals and compare.
Estimate how long it takes to complete a task manually/with a machine.
Measure space needed to complete certain physical activities (for example standing, running, hopping).

Society
Collect pictures of sports people—compare their lifestyles to yours.
Discuss tasks families do daily—illustrate; indicate high and low energy use for each.

Interview people in the school about their use of machines—could they do the same job without them?

List questions to ask grandparents about the use of technology in their childhood—invite them in, ask them to bring photographs.

Visit a pioneer museum—find evidence of the energy used most.

Science

Use marbles to explore moving energy; drop one into a group of other marbles—what happens?

Predict which energy source is used most frequently in the school over a week; record daily usage.

Check and compare your pulse after high/low energy activities.

Use the bottom of a paper cup, make a hole in it, pull a balloon through it, blow it up— let it go in water!

Environment

Observe traffic near your school; note exhaust emission—do some produce more than others?

Draw a poster of things that use energy in your home.

Make up lists of how energy can be conserved in each room of the house.

Cut local temperature reports from newspapers—indicate at what temperature you would wear a jumper/jacket to school.

Art

Make a mobile of things powered by a specific energy source, for example, car—petrol.

Make a poster collage depicting energy use at home.

Do a large painting of the sun; surround with pictures of life.

Use different colours to make a design conveying heat/warmth/light.

Make a collage of summer fabrics.

Music

Listen to and compare traditional and modern electronic music (for example Bach, Beethoven and Vangelis).

Play musical instruments that produce music solely by movement (for example bells).

List, examine musical instruments—discuss energy sources.

Make musical chimes using driftwood and sea-shells.

Health

List food eaten daily; graph, showing calorie/kilojule values.
What 'fuel' does your body need? Have someone trace around your body on paper—paste pictures of healthy food inside.
Identify high/low energy food—discuss body fuel consumption.
Make lists of food you like/dislike—how do they rate as energy sources?

Technology

Cut pictures of machines out of magazines, label with energy sources.
Invent a machine with a funny use (for example to tie shoe laces); make it out of scrap materials—what renewable energy will power it?
Bring simple machines from home, label and display.
Use boxes/scrap materials to make a house which is solar powered.
Make a weather vane; use cotton reel, a block of wood, drinking straw and foil.

Science and energy: Section B

Exploring heat

Expectations are that children:
- become aware of the presence of heat
- become aware of the importance of heat for life and growth

○ **Resources:** Open space, notebooks, pencils, large sheets of paper, textas, blackboard, chalk
Skills: Recording, reporting, comparing, discussing
Concepts: Differences in temperature, heat—indoor/outdoor insulation

(a)

1 *Teacher talk: What is heat? Can you see/touch it? Is there some in this room?*

Children become scientists and make a report about indoor heat.
Teacher talk: Are there places/things that are warmer/colder?
How can you tell if something is warm/hot/cold?

Partners explore the room, discuss and record indicators of heat.

2 In the class group, scientists share their findings. List on a poster places (or things) that were warmer (for example near a sunny window, near a heater).

3 Scientists walk in other rooms/areas of the school and note changes in temperature.
Teacher talk: Are some areas (office, corridors) warmer/cooler than others? Why?

Activities (a) and (b) have a follow-through theme and can be taught in sequence or alone.

Encourage children to reflect on things that retain/provide warmth, for example clothing, house insulation, air-conditioning.

○ **Resources:** Classroom, outdoors
Skills: Recording, predicting, comparing
Concepts: Effects of heat—objects/living things, weather, differences in temperature, insulation

(b)

1 Children in role of scientists record evidence of heat.
Teacher talk: Are some places warmer than others?
Draw attention to the effects of heat on objects/living things.
Children observe living things—remind them that growth depends on heat.

2 Discuss and compare cold and warm weather.
Teacher talk: Is heat present when it is cold? How do you know?
What do you do to become warm in cold weather?
Children improvise what they do to keep warm/create heat.

○ **Resources:** Open space
Skills: Suggesting, discussing, inferring, forming conclusions
Concepts: Heat, life, growth, seasons

(a)

1 *Teacher talk: What vegetables/fruit grow in warm/hot weather.*

Record children's suggestions.

Resources: Open space
Skills: Discussing, hypothesising, forming conclusions
Concepts: Effect of heat on growth, sources of heat, solar energy

Children become a fruit/vegetable and mime the process of growth from blossom to the ripened fruit.
Encourage the action by commenting on the sun's warmth and the different stages of growth.

2 Discuss what might happen if the same fruit/vegetable did not have enough heat. Have children reflect on the importance of the right amount of heat for growth/survival.

(b)

1 Children become market gardeners who grow tomatoes. In groups ask them to work out how they can grow tomatoes in colder months.
Teacher talk: *What will the tomato plants need to grow (air, food, water, heat)?*

Discuss the balance needed for successful growth.

2 As the market gardeners plant their seedlings circulate and ask focusing questions in role of supervisor.
Teacher talk: *Will your plants get enough sun in that spot?*
How will they live through the very cold weather?
How can you keep your plants warm to help them grow?

Comment on sources of heat to guide children.

3 Organise a meeting of market gardeners to report on successes or failures. Discuss the use of glass-houses.

The effects of heat

Expectations are that children:
- understand that heat can produce changes
- become aware of differences in temperature

Resources: Open space, story: 'The sun and the wind'
Skills: Discussing, problem-solving, observing, comparing
Concepts: Effects of heat, changes made by heat, heat sources

1 Read: 'The sun and the wind'. The class act out the story. All can be involved with several children taking the roles of the sun and the wind.

2 Discuss how the heat affected the person.
Teacher talk: *What happens to:*
—your body if you're too hot?
—your icecream if you don't eat it quickly?

Children suggest other things affected by heat.
Discuss how heat changes these things.
Children mime the changes in things affected by heat, for example melting ice/butter/chocolate or cooking meat/rice.

3 Observe the effects of heat from the sun outdoors, for example blistering paint, faded awnings, dried grasses/plants. Compare the effect of the sun's heat and other sources such as stoves, wood fires and so on.

Resources: Open space
Skills: Discussing, problem-solving
Concepts: Changes made by heat, effects of heat on life/growth

1 Organise children into groups. One child is a chicken farmer and the others are eggs.
Teacher talk: There are no mother hens around! How can the eggs hatch? What can the chicken farmer do to help?
2 Groups discuss the problem then act out their solution.

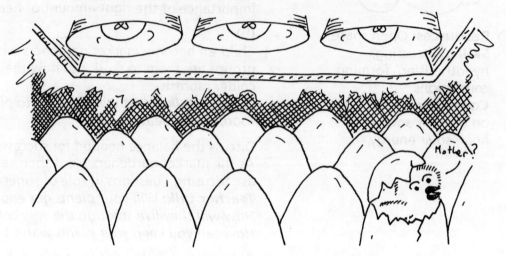

3 Groups perform their solution to the class. Encourage the audience to comment on the effectiveness of solutions. Discuss the changes heat will have on the eggs.

Resources: Open space
Skills: Hypothesising, predicting, discussing, suggesting
Concepts: Changes of state, expansion, temperature

1 With partners children become:
   (a) a cake baking in the oven
Teacher talk: You've just been put in the oven. Slowly show what happens as the oven gets warmer. What is happening to you?
   (b) an egg in a saucepan filled with water
Teacher talk: The stove is getting warmer, and warmer! Show what happens to the water when it is very hot? What is happening to the egg?

Discuss the effects of heat expansion. Children suggest other situations in which heat expansion occurs.

Resources: Open space
Skills: Predicting, responding
Concepts: Heat variation/presence

1 In groups of three, children mime the melting rate of a small ice cube in one of the following situations:
   (a) inside the refrigerator (not the freezer compartment)
   (b) on the window-sill on a sunny day
   (c) in a frypan on a hot stove
Teacher talk: In which place is there more heat? Is there any heat in the refrigerator?

Remind children that heat exists even when it is cold.
2 Use real ice-blocks to prove children's predictions.

Changing temperatures—changing lifestyles

Expectations are that children:
- have an understanding of how climate affects lifestyles
- identify clothing to suit different temperatures

○□ **Resources:** Open space, sheet of paper, cards with names of seasons, magazines, scissors, glue
Skills: Discussing, forming conclusions
Concepts: Seasons, climate, temperature, weather

1 Discuss and list activities children are involved in (that is sport/recreational).
2 Organise children into groups of four or five. Each group is given a card with a season written on it. Groups discuss an activity appropriate to the season.
Teacher talk: What kind of activity is it?
Is it only done at that time of year?
Do you wear special clothing for it?
Do you use any kind of equipment?
Discuss. Groups improvise the activity.

3 Groups perform the activity to the class. The audience identifies the season the activity takes place in.
Teacher talk: When would you usually go on a picnic?
What time of year is tennis/soccer played in?
Would a person's clothing tell you what season it is?

If necessary groups assist by saying what they are wearing.
4 Cut pictures of people from magazines. Sort into seasons according to the clothing worn and paste on a poster.

○□ **Resources:** Open space, classroom furniture
Skills: Discussing, describing, comparing, hypothesising
Concepts: Influence of climate/environment on lifestyle/housing

1 Children pretend they live in different parts of the world, for example:
 —in a hot desert
 —a tropical rain-forest
 —a land with ice and snow
 —a city/suburb like their own
Children suggest other places they could live in.
Teacher talk: What kind of climate does each place have?
Would people living there wear similar clothing? Why/Why not?
Would houses be different in each place? Discuss.
2 Organise children into groups according to the environment they choose to live in. Using classroom furniture and scrap materials groups build houses to suit their environment/climate.
3 Each group describes their house and gives reasons for its suitability to a particular climate.

4 In their house children improvise a family preparing for the day's activities. (Firstly groups define their roles and decide on appropriate clothing for the activities.)

5 Children report on their experiences to the class. Make comparisons between groups.
Teacher talk: *Why were you wearing a coat while Alana was only wearing a T-shirt?*
If you were in a hot/cold climate how would you keep cool/warm?
Why did your family have hot porridge for breakfast and Jenni's family have cereal with cold milk?

Have children reflect on whether climate influences lifestyle (for example housing, activities, clothing, food).

Resources: An assortment of hats, shoes, clothing
Skills: Hypothesising, identifying, forming conclusions
Concepts: Climate influences dress

1 Children sit around an assortment of clothing and accessories. Each child chooses an item to wear. Children think of the climate in which it might be worn and the person who might wear it.

2 Children act out the person and do the activity appropriate to the clothing worn, for example:
—rubber boots—a child walking home from school on a wet day
—straw hat—a woman enjoying the sun on the beach

3 Individuals perform their roles for the class. The audience identifies the weather/climate and the character.

Heat activities across the curriculum

Language
Write 'warm'/'hot' words on a cut-out of the sun.
Write fruit/vegetable stories:
  'I am a red tomato.'
  'The biggest apple in the world.'
Write a rhyming verse about your favourite time of year.
Send letters to people living in different climates; ask about their weather.
Read/write about fire-breathing dragons.
Write words rhyming with 'heat'.
List words describing heat on a poster and illustrate.
Write about a chick in its shell: should it feel safe/warm?

Mathematics
Make a graph of hours of sunshine in a week.

Do some cooking—estimate the time it takes to cook eggs/peas.

Weigh half a cup of butter, melt it—has the weight changed?

Put water in a saucepan, measure the level, boil it for five minutes, measure again.

Examine instruments that measure temperature; think of other ways to measure temperature.

Society

Collect travel brochures of other countries—determine their climate.

Name famous sports-people—what season/climate do they play in?

Make a seasons poster of clothing.

Visit people who use heat in their jobs—hairdresser, baker, welder.

Look through the telephone book, find industries supplying heating fuels—write to them for information.

Draw a plan of your street, draw/cut out buildings showing size and number of windows, paste on plan—which use more natural light/heat?

Walk in the neighbourhood, note houses with chimneys— are they being used? What time of year are they used most?

Science

Estimate/test temperatures of three glasses of water: on window-sill, in the outdoors sun/shade.

Put objects made from different materials in hot water for two minutes. Which retains heat longer?

Make two mixtures for pancakes, one with self-raising flour, the other without; compare the cooked pancakes.

How many different ways can you start a fire? Illustrate on a poster.

Environment

Plant the same kind of seeds in two pots; put one in a shady spot, the other in full sun—which will show first signs of growth?

Draw a shady/sunny environment.

Draw environments of different climates, label descriptively.

Visit local gardens; list things growing well in full sun.

Visit a plant nursery—what vegetables/fruit are recommended for planting in summer/autumn?

Discuss ozone layer damage—how does this affect Earth?

How do animals respond to climate, for example hibernation?

Art
Make a sun mobile with cardboard shapes of things to do with heat.

Save seeds from vegetables; make an environmental collage.

Using a single sheet of card make a hat to wear while you watch tennis.

Choose and mix colours to paint pictures expressing warmth/heat.

Melt crayons/candles and drip onto sheet, paint over.

Music
Fill three identical glasses with water of different temperatures, that is icy cold, hot, tap water—strike out a tune with a fork. Are there differences in the sound of each?

Look at newspaper entertainment pages—are musical events held in outdoor venues? Does climate have a bearing on this?

Health
Draw clothing suitable for different seasons.

Draw a seasonal activity clock.

Have a fashion parade of safe summer fashions.

Visit the school canteen—what are the most popular summer/winter foods?

What do senses tell you about heat?

Discuss how you look after pets in hot weather.

List and draw clothing that protects you from the sun.

Make unusual hats for protection from the sun.

Discuss fire safety in your school; invite the fire brigade to visit.

Technology
Design unusual umbrellas to protect things from the sun, for example a car, an elephant.

Built a house from scrap materials to suit hot/cold climates.

Draw/construct model barbecues, fireplaces with scrap materials; write captions describing fuel used and pollution potential of each.

Science and technology

Science and technology

Exploring the concept of work
Expectations are that children:
- identify work and leisure
- compare paid and unpaid work

Resources: Open space, classroom, alarm clock, classroom furniture and equipment
Skills: Responding, inferring, identifying, discussing, forming conclusions
Concepts: Work—household tasks/occupations, paid/unpaid work

1 Children pretend they are sleeping. It is early morning. The alarm clock rings. Children get up and get ready for work.
Teacher talk: *What work do you do?*
Do you wear special clothes for your job?
Do you use tools/equipment?
Will you need to take anything with you?
2 Children create their work environment using available furniture and classroom equipment then act out their job situation in the structure.
3 After the improvisation discuss the concept of work.
Teacher talk: *What is work?*
What do you do when you are working?
How do you know that it is work?
4 Children identify and discuss other work activities done by people at home, for example cleaning the house, doing the gardening, etc. Individuals mime one of these tasks.
5 Children return to the class group. Ask what difference there is between this work and the work they improvised. Encourage children to think about payment, organisation of the work situation and whose expectations are being met.

Resources: Open space/classroom, pictures of people working
Skills: Discussing
Concepts: Work—paid/unpaid/volunteer, leisure activities, expectations, wages/salaries

Activities (a) and (b) have a follow-through theme and can be taught in sequence or alone.

(a)
1 Use pictures of people in work situations (paid/unpaid, volunteer) and leisure activities to set up an art exhibition. (Children could frame pictures cut from magazines.)
2 In role of art gallery manager tell children that you need workers to set up the art exhibition. Discuss your expectations as employer.
Teacher talk: *The exhibition has to be set up by this afternoon.*
It's ten o'clock—I want the exhibition ready by one o'clock. I'll pay you $2.00 an hour.
3 Children become the workers setting up the exhibition. Circulate as the manager commenting on and guiding the work.

○□△ **Resources:** Open
space/classroom, pictures
of people working (as
above), poster card, textas
Skills: Discussing,
categorising, defining
Concepts: Work/leisure,
paid/unpaid work, work
expectations/purpose

4 When the exhibition is ready workers collect their pay.
   *Teacher talk: You've been very quick—its only half-past
   twelve.*
   You can have a bonus of $5.00 for finishing early.
   How much do I owe you altogether?
5 In the class children discuss their work roles and the gallery
   manager's expectations. Ask the class to suggest a title for
   the exhibition which reflects the theme of the pictures.

(b)
1 With partners children become visitors to the 'Work and
   Recreation' exhibition. Encourage them to talk to each other
   about the activities in each picture.
   *Teacher talk: Does the picture show work/leisure activities?
   How do you know?
   Who is the work being done for? (self, others)
   Do you think the person is paid for this work?
   Why is the person doing the work?*
2 Ask children to categorise specific pictures (for example paid,
   volunteer, leisure, chores, etc.). Write cards for each category
   and place as section headings around the room.
3 As gallery manager tell workers that the pictures need to be
   rearranged. In pairs workers put pictures under the
   appropriate section headings.
4 With the whole class, assess the re-arranged exhibition.

○□△ **Resources:** Open
space/classroom
Skills: Responding,
defining, categorising
Concepts: Work/leisure—
result/reward/
accomplishment/purpose

1 Individuals name a leisure activity their parents do, for
   example:
   —fishing
   —sport
   —painting
   —sewing
   Children mime the activity.
2 Select individuals to perform the mime to the class.
   *Teacher talk: Why is Jim fishing/playing tennis?
   Is it work?*
3 Organise children into groups of four or five to discuss one of
   the activities presented.
   *Teacher talk: What happened when the activity was
   performed?
   Was anything made? (result/accomplished)
   What did Jim get from doing the activity? (reward)
   Is it work or leisure?*

   Discuss.
4 Children mime the activity again but this time pretend that it
   is work, for example fishing/playing tennis to earn an income.
   Define what aspects need to be present to categorise an
   activity as 'work' or 'leisure'.

Designing machines

Expectations are that children:
- become aware that need and creativity are required for the invention of machines
- identify the uses of different machines

○ **Resources:** Pictures of machines, fiction/non-fiction books on machines, paper and pencils
Skills: Reporting, forming conclusions
Concepts: Machine design/use/purpose

(a)

1 Show pictures of machines frequently used in our daily lives, for example hairdryer, vacuum cleaner, lawn mower, computer, fan.
2 The class lists the tasks performed by the machines for example hairdryer—dries hair, fan—cools the room. Individuals mime doing the task before the machine was invented.
3 Children become the inventors of the machines. In role, children select a task from the list and design the appropriate machine for it. Remind children that they need to show the inside workings as well as what it looks like when completed.
4 Children explain their designs at a meeting of inventors.

○ **Resources:** Classroom, large sheet paper, textas, scrap materials, glue, masking tape, scissors
Skills: Discussing, hypothesising, problem-solving, creating, inventing, designing, predicting
Concepts: Machine design/use/purpose

(b)

1 *Teacher talk: Think of a small/large/quiet/noisy machine.*

Children make suggestions.
Partners make a machine for a specific task using their bodies and adding appropriate movements and sound.
2 In the class group, discuss the usefulness of the machines.
Teacher talk: What did it do?
Can the task be completed without the machine?
How much time would it take?
3 *Teacher talk: Chores can be tedious, can't they!*
Wouldn't it be great if machines could do your jobs for you!
What jobs do you have to do?

Write a class list of chores children do.
4 Have children pretend they are inventors who design machines for tasks listed. Encourage inventors to use a variety of materials to design/make a model of their machine.

Activities (a) and (b) have a follow-through theme and can be taught in sequence or alone.

Resources: Classroom, scrap materials, glue, masking tape, scissors
Skills: Discussing, designing, inventing, creating, forming conclusions
Concepts: Inventing for specific needs, creativity/ originality

1 Assume the role of the Queen speaking to a group of inventors.
Teacher talk: I've called you to my palace for an urgent job. My collection of rare live butterflies has escaped. You must invent a machine to find and catch them unharmed.

The Queen brings in a variety of materials (real). Ask the inventors if there is any information they want to know about the butterflies before they begin the task, for example how big and how many there are.

2 Inventors in pairs confer over the task and begin.
3 On completion the inventions are presented to the Queen.
Teacher talk: All the machines are different—why? Can they all do the same job?

Discuss in terms of individuals' abilities and creativity! Conclude that people's creativity is unique to each individual.

Work environments

Expectations are that children:
- understand the nature of work environments
- compare work environments
- become aware that work environments have standards of safety

Resources: Open space
Skills: Responding, discussing, describing, comparing, forming conclusions
Concepts: Work— places/situations, similarities/differences

1 *Teacher talk: Is this school a work environment? Who is it a work environment for? What other places do people work in?*

Discuss briefly.
2 Organise children into groups of four or five. Each group selects a work environment to discuss in terms of what happens in it, who works there and what equipment is used. Circulate among groups posing questions and making suggestions if required.
3 Groups improvise the work situation. Remind children to define their roles first.
4 Groups perform their improvisation to the class. Have the class make comparisons between the work situations, determine what they all have in common and what makes it a work environment.

Resources: Classroom, furniture/equipment, scrap materials, glue, scissors, masking tape
Skills: Suggesting, problem-solving, creating, designing
Concepts: Product, manufacture, safety standards, work practices, protective clothing

1 Tell children to set up a work environment where machines are manufactured.
2 The class makes suggestions of what they could invent, for example:
   'Something to turn the pages of a book.'
   In pairs children decide what they will invent and report back to the class group. Partners set up the work environment to make the product using classroom furniture and equipment.
3 Before the improvisation begins, assume the role of 'Safety Officer' and inspect the manufacturing outlets. During the inspection ask questions relating to safety standards.
   Teacher talk: Do you need protective clothing?
   What will you do in case of accident/fire?

   Draw attention to 'structures' which may be unsafe. Ask workers to rectify the problem and inspect again.
4 Workers select from a variety of scrap materials and begin the manufacturing task. In role as manager circulate giving encouragement and advice where needed.
5 Workers present their finished product, commenting on its usefulness and pointing out safety features.

Technology activities across the curriculum

Language
Make a motorcar shape; write describing words in it.
List words to do with making/creating.
Cut pictures of machines from catalogues, write descriptive verbs, for example electric mixer—rotates.
Write a poem beginning:
   'Off to work we go. . .!'

Read books on the history of machines.
Make machine noises using digraphs or vowel sounds.
Write stories on:
   'I am a machine'
   'Leisure Island'

Mathematics

Do a task—how much time would it take two people to do it?
Work out an hourly rate for a particular job.
Measure the dimensions of machines used at school.
List ways in which technology is used to work out mathematics, for example calculators, scales, computers, etc.
Observe wind-up toys; estimate/check how long they run after being wound.

Society

Research machines used in rural societies.
Research lives of famous inventors, for example Leonardo da Vinci.
Draw/design clothing for various work situations.
Invite a volunteer worker to visit, for example 'Meals on wheels'.
Set up a hobbies display; invite other classes to view.
Draw modes of transport used for family outings.
Visit a manufacturing business with an assembly line.
Find/draw pictures of mechanical things used by people for leisure, for example things in an amusement park.

Science

Experiment with different ways of doing the same job. Which is quicker?
Place small machine parts (cogs, wheels) on coloured paper on a window-sill; remove items after two weeks—what has happened?
Make a bridge with cardboard; use an empty egg-shell to support it, place books on top of it—how many can you put on before the shell breaks?

Environment

How does technology contribute to pollution?
Noise pollution—what causes it?
List commonly used machines—what materials are used to make them?
Design a motorcar which uses solar energy.
Find out about composting; draw a composting machine; write directions for its use.

Art

Trace around cogs, wheels, small machine parts.
Make a sculpture using small machine parts.
Paint, decorate old machine parts and display.
Draw/paint/make space-age machines.
Visit an art gallery to view a multi-media exhibition.
Make a mosaic collage with pictures of machines from magazines.

Music

Use parts of broken machines as percussion instruments.
Create a machine noise 'symphony' using vocal sounds.
Collect/sing songs about travelling on 'machines', for example:
    'The wheels of the bus'
    'Sailing up the river on a sunny afternoon'.
Visit a museum of music.
Compose a song with a work theme.

Health

Invite an industrial safety officer to speak to the class.
Discuss a visit to the dentist—what machines does he use?
What is a life-saving machine?
Discuss cleanliness/hygiene—what machines are used to keep homes clean.
Visit local work environments.
List garden tools; illustrate.
What rules in your school make it a happy, healthy work/play environment?

Technology

Construct a tent frame with popsticks.
Look at shapes of roofs in the local area; draw/make model frames of roofs using popsticks.
Use Meccano or Lego Technics sets to construct.
Make bridges out of scrap materials—test their strength.
Make a bridge out of one piece of cardboard—put things on it to see how strong it is.
Set up a 'tinker table' where children can pull old machines apart.

Mathematics

| Mathematics: Section A | Exploring maths |

Mathematics: Section A

Exploring maths

Expectations are that children:
- become aware that maths occurs as part of daily life

Resources: Classroom, pictures of workers (baker, hairdresser, bricklayer, etc.)

Concepts: Cardinal number, addition, estimation, quantity, comparison, money value.

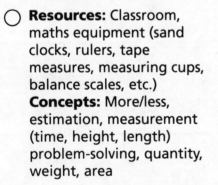

1 **Teacher talk:** *What is maths?*
Maths is used in lots of ways!
How are people in the pictures using maths?
2 Children become workers, form same occupation groups and discuss their jobs. Circulate and ask focus questions.
Teacher talk: *What kind of job do you do?*
How do you do it?
What do you use in your job?
3 Groups improvise the work situation, then show their group work to the class.
Encourage the audience to ask maths related questions.
Teacher talk: *How many kinds of fruit/vegetables do you sell?*
Do you sell by weight/quantity?
What is your most expensive item?
How heavy is your biggest vegetable?
How much does it cost?
How much would two cost, etc.?

In their groups children discuss, record responses and report to the class.
4 Have children reflect on the nature of maths in work situations, for example factories, offices, farms. Improvise specific tasks from these. Conclude that maths is used by many people in their work.

Resources: Classroom, maths equipment (sand clocks, rulers, tape measures, measuring cups, balance scales, etc.)

Concepts: More/less, estimation, measurement (time, height, length) problem-solving, quantity, weight, area

1 **Teacher talk:** *We know that people use maths every day.*
How is maths used in your home?

List children's suggestions, for example making a cake, hanging a picture, setting the table.
2 Choose individuals to mime a task from the list. Ask the class to identify the mathematics involved in each.
Teacher talk: *(Making a cake) How big will it be?*
What size mixing bowl will you need?
How many eggs? How much flour/sugar?
What should the oven temperature be?

(Hanging a picture) How big/heavy is it?
How much space will you need for its size?
How high will it be hung?

3 Children improvise tasks using maths equipment to show an aspect of the mathematics involved, for example a ruler or arbitrary measure to work out how high the picture should be; scales/measuring cups for cake ingredients, etc.

○ **Resources:** Classroom, classroom furniture/ equipment, paper, pencils
Concepts: Problem-solving, logic, measurement, (height, length, comparative measure) estimation, addition, subtraction

(a)

1 *Teacher talk: What if a magic wind came and took away our maths equipment?*
Could we still do maths?
Let's find out.

Children personify the wind and carry away the maths equipment to a designated space where it becomes 'invisible'.

2 Children return to the class group.
Teacher talk: Let's do a measuring lesson.
Get the maths equipment we need to measure the classroom furniture.

Children 'discover' all the equipment gone and search for it with 'negative' results.

3 *Teacher talk: Can we measure the desks/chairs without maths equipment?*
Encourage children to find other classroom materials which can be used for the task.
In pairs children discuss, complete and record the task.

4 In the class group, individuals report on how the task was completed. Ascertain if children are aware of the need for uniformity of materials for accuracy.
Teacher talk: Why did Sue use more units than John to measure the same chair?
If she used the same kind of units would her measure be the same?
Is it important that the units you are measuring with be the same size?

5 *Teacher talk: Can you solve other maths tasks without equipment?*
Children nominate and complete other tasks. Encourage a variety of tasks so that different maths skills are used, for example:
 —addition and subtraction—use tables, chairs, pencils, books
 —space—use books to work out the area of a desk
 —mass—make weight comparisons of hand-held objects

6 Children reflect on the most efficient and accurate way of completing mathematical tasks. (Responses will vary depending on individual mathematical experiences.)
Teacher talk: Would a large/small unit be quicker to measure with?

Activities (a) and (b) have a follow-through theme and can be taught in sequence or alone.

What would be the quickest/more efficient way of measuring length?
Guide children to conclude that maths equipment can be a practical and efficient way of solving maths problems.

Resources: Classroom, maths equipment, notebooks and pencils
Concepts: Patterning, problem-solving, smallest, biggest, sequence, ordering, grouping, notation

(b)

1 *Teacher talk: Let's get our maths equipment back from the magic wind!*
We'll become detectives and look for clues.
Did you know that the wind leaves patterns wherever it goes!

Detectives look for patterns on walls, ceilings, shelving, furniture, materials and record patterns seen.
2 They report their findings at a meeting of detectives. Direct focus to the recorded patterns.
Teacher talk: How do we know that it is a pattern?
Where does your pattern start?
Where does the sequence begin again?
How many groups in the pattern?
What is the number of your pattern?
If all the groups were added together what would be the total number of the pattern?
3 *Teacher talk: The magic wind must like patterns.*
If we give it our patterns it might return our maths equipment.

Have children paste their pattern on a poster in order from the shortest to the longest, or from the smallest pattern number to the largest.
4 The detectives form a circle and place the completed poster in the centre. One by one children call back the magic wind by reading out their pattern number (for example 2-3-2, 2-3-2 or 1-2, 1-2).
5 Children close their eyes while the wind takes the poster away.
(Remove the poster).
In role as the wind children return the maths equipment.

Resources: Classroom, poster paper, pencils, maths equipment
Concepts: Comparative measure, estimation, addition, measurement of height and length, interval counting, more/less

1 *Teacher talk: You are a two-headed monster.*
You have twice as many eyes, arms, legs, feet as you have now.
How many eyes/arms/legs/feet will that be?
Can you count in groups of two?
Can you show what you look like?
Children join up with a partner to become the monster.
2 *Teacher talk: Now that you are two times as big could you sit in one chair comfortably?*
3 Monsters try sitting. Monsters estimate how much wider the desk/chair needs to be. Children draw or make an outline on the floor with maths materials to show the required size.

Resources: Classroom, pencils, crepe or tissue paper, scissors, glue, masking tape

Concepts: One-to-one correspondence, addition, notation, grouping, cardinal number.

1 *Teacher talk: Pretend you are a two-headed monster. The queen has invited you to her palace. What will you wear? Have a look in your wardrobe?*

With a partner children become the monster and look through the wardrobe.
Teacher talk: How many pairs of shoes/socks will you need? What other things will you wear? Take out everything you need.

Children make with paper, the items of clothing they will wear.

2 Children record the total number of clothing items needed and group according to sets, for example:
Teacher talk: How many pairs of shoes will your monster need? How many shoes will that be altogether?

3 Partners put on imaginary clothing and get ready to visit the queen.
The monsters model their 'finery'.

Sorting and grouping

Expectations are that children:
- identify criteria for sorting into groups
- recognise the number of groups

Resources: Open space, poster paper, textas

Concepts: Ordinal number, attribute identification, developing criteria for sorting/sequencing, problem-solving

1 *Teacher talk: Pretend you are a circus performer. What kind of performer would you like to be?*

List suggestions. Each child chooses a role.

2 Select four or five leaders to represent different performing groups. Children sort themselves into the group they best fit (for example animal acts, trapeze artists or clowns).
In groups children discuss roles and decide on a group performing name.

3 In role as ringmaster call a meeting of groups. Tell the performers that you need information for the program.
Teacher talk: What is your group called? Why do you belong to that group? (criteria) What is the number of each group? How many groups altogether? Which is the largest/smallest group?

Record group names and responses.

4 Teacher talk: *The show always opens with a parade.*
Which act should be first?
Who should go second, third, fourth, etc?

Record the number order next to the group name.
Groups organise themselves according to order.
Have children rehearse the parade around the circus ring.

Resources: Large space, string
Concepts: more, less, attribute identification, sorting

1 Teacher talk: *Pretend you are a space creature.*
You have only one arm or leg.

Children say whether they have either one arm or leg and what colour they are.
The space creatures float around the room.

2 Tell the creatures that they like meeting up with others who look the same.
On the 'freeze' signal children stop, find others who have the same colour and number of limbs, join up and move in space together.

3 Gather the creatures around a large circle on the floor made with a piece of string.
Ask one creature to enter the circle and name its attributes (for example I am green. I have two legs, one arm, one head.)
All creatures with the same attributes enter the circle.

4 Make sorting more complex by adding an overlapping circle into which creatures are sorted by one or more criteria.
Creatures not fitting into any of the circles remain outside.

Resources: Open space
Concepts: Attribute identification, sorting, addition, logic, estimation, height, length, width, size comparison

1 Teacher talk: *Pretend you are a zoo animal.*
What kind of animal are you?
Are you big or small?

Children select roles and organise themselves into animal groups according to certain criteria—either the animal's physical characteristics and/or habits.

2 Divide the working space into enclosures.
The animal groups choose and enter their enclosure.
Teacher talk: How big/small is your area?
Can you estimate how wide/long?
Is the area big enough for an animal your size?
How high/long is the fence?

3 Circulate in role as zoo-keeper questioning children about criteria used to form their groups.
Teacher talk: What is the same about animals in your group?
Do you look the same?
Are you the same size?
Do you move as quickly/slowly?
Do you like to eat the same kind of things?

4 Children return to the class and group members say what criteria was used to form groups.
Encourage comments from the audience on the appropriateness of criteria.

5 Individuals draw a picture of themselves as the animal and paste it on a poster in the appropriate grouping.
Record the number for each group and responses relating to criteria.

Resources: Classroom, letters from the Magic Numero, classroom maths equipment, coloured paper, textas, pencils, streamers, art/craft materials, scissors, glue
Concepts: sorting, grouping, counting, cardinal number

1 *Teacher talk: I've just found a letter on my desk from someone called the Magic Numero.*

Read the letter to the class.

Dear teacher and class,

Please come 2 my birthday party at the Mansion of Numbers on (date) at (time). B4 you come you must find groups of numbers and send them 2 me.
Here are some clues 2 help you:
Find things 2 sort into groups.
Count 2 find the number in a group.
Look 4 numbers you cannot see.
Collect the numbers & leave them in the front office.
Happy number hunting!
Love from 'The Magic Numero!'

2 Discuss the letter.
Teacher talk: What does the Magic Numero want you to do?
What does 'numbers you cannot see'* mean?

(*Note: This refers to the cardinal number of sets/groups—the number is 'unseen' until the objects in the group are counted.)

Children look for things that can be grouped (for example shapes of the same size/colour, books in the same series, coloured pencils, etc.).

3 Walk around guiding children to materials which can be sorted/grouped.

Teacher talk: Can you make a group with these things?
Do they belong together? Why?
What is the group number?

4 Children record their grouping experiences and share findings with the class.

Teacher talk: Do you think we've done what the Magic Numero asked?
How did you find the number of a group? (count)
Repeat steps 2 and 3 for more sorting and grouping experiences if necessary.

5 Respond to the Magic Numero's letter and send the children's recorded work.

6 Prepare a response to the class and have it 'arrive' a day or so later, for example:

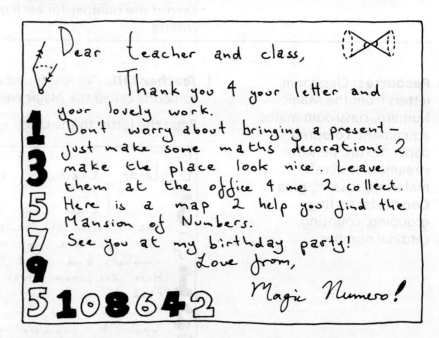

Dear teacher and class,
Thank you 4 your letter and your lovely work.
Don't worry about bringing a present — Just make some maths decorations 2 make the place look nice. Leave them at the office 4 me 2 collect. Here is a map 2 help you find the Mansion of Numbers.
See you at my birthday party!
Love from,
Magic Numero!

1 3 5 7 9 5 1 0 8 6 4 2

Include a map of the school grounds showing where the party* will take place.
(*The party should be organised without children's knowledge by parents or helpers. Food arrangements could fit in with the group theme).

7 Children create decorations which fit the mathematical theme, for example paper chains, shape mobiles, paper flowers with the petal number written in the centre.
Choose children to deliver them to the 'office' for the Magic Numero.

Fractions

Expectations are that children:
- develop an understanding that a fraction is part of a whole number or quantity
- are able to show fractions, halves and quarters

Resources: Open space
Concepts: Subtraction, addition, size comparison, quantity, one-to-one correspondence, problem-solving

1 **Teacher talk:** *Dinosaurs are pretty big aren't they?*
Would a dinosaur fit in our room?
How big would a dinosaur's birthday cake be?
Do we have enough helpers to make a dinosaur's birthday cake?
We need a huge mixing bowl!

The class forms a circle to represent the bowl. Children put the ingredients in and make the sound of a giant electric mixer stirring the ingredients.

2 Have children join hands and pretend they are the cake just out of the oven.
Walk around the circle and cut through joined hands to make each child a slice of cake.
Teacher talk: *How many pieces of cake are there?*
If everyone got a piece would there be enough?
Would there be a piece for the dinosaur?
Let's see how much the dinosaur wants to eat.

A child in role of the dinosaur eats some pieces of cake.
Remind the dinosaur to mind its manners and eat one piece at the time (remove a child for each slice eaten).
Teacher talk: *How many pieces did the dinosaur eat?*
How many pieces left?
How many children would get a piece of cake now?
How many would miss out?

4 Children take turns as the dinosaur eating the cake.

Resources: Classroom, magazines, scissors, rulers, pencils
Concepts: Whole, part of, equal number, halves

Activities (a) and (b) have a follow-through theme and can be taught in sequence or alone.

(a)
1 In pairs children select a picture from a magazine, cut it out and display it.
2 Partners show part of the picture to the class in tableau form, for example, a person watering a plant under a verandah—one child becomes the plant, the other is the person watering (the verandah is not shown).
Draw children's attention to the whole picture and ask which part was not shown.

3 Children form groups of equal number.
Groups select a picture and present it in tableau form to the class. Each child says what part of the picture they are.
Teacher talk: What parts of the picture were shown?
What parts are missing?
What needs to be added to make up the whole picture?

Resources: Classroom, magazine pictures, rulers, textas, scissors
Concepts: Halves of number/quantity, straight lines, squares

(b)
1 Partners select a magazine picture and cut it in halves.
Collect the children's pictures.
2 Divide children into two groups.
The groups sit opposite each other.
Teacher talk: How many halves make up our whole class?
How many children in half of our class?
Does one half have the same number as the other?
3 Redistribute the pictures giving each child half.
Choose individuals to figurate/mime things in their half of the picture and say what they are, for example:
I am a palm tree.
Now I am the pot that the tree is in.
I'm the coconut in the tree.
Whoever has the other half of the picture then comes forward and presents the other half to make the whole picture.

Resources: Open space, coloured paper, rulers, textas, adhesive tape
Concepts: equal groups, problem-solving, halves, quarters, subtraction, cardinal number.

1 Children imagine they are strawberries in a garden bed and improvise the following story:
Teacher talk: The Strawberries are growing proudly in their little garden bed.
The Sunbeams tickle their red heads.
They are happy and warm and grow just a little bit more each day.
It's night-time now.
Uh, oh! Here come the Frosties.
They pinch and bite the Strawberries.
The Strawberries shiver with cold.
They huddle close together to keep warm.
Then it's morning, the Sunbeams come again.
They are glad!
But sometimes, if the Frosties have been very nasty, some Strawberries die.
The Green People who care for them are sad.
How can they help the strawberries?
2 Tell the children that the gentle Green People want to help solve the problem.
Teacher talk: How can they help the Strawberries?
If you were cold in your bed at night what would you do to get warm?

3 Discuss the characters in the story. Children work out how many groups are needed to represent the characters. Children form groups representing the Strawberries, the Sunbeams, the Frosties and the Green People. Groups discuss then act out the story.
(The Green People need to think about how they can protect the Strawberries).

4 In the class group, discuss how the Green People solved the problem. In role as Green People the class makes a patchwork quilt to cover the Strawberries.
Each child selects a square piece of coloured paper and marks it in halves/quarters with bright coloured textas.

5 Children join the squares carefully over the strawberry patch to make a quilt and sit around it.
Teacher talk: How many parts were used to make the whole quilt?
Can you find half/quarter of the whole quiit?
How many fractions in half/quarter?
If I took away ten fractions from the whole quilt how many would be left, etc.?
If two strawberry patches had to be covered how many coloured squares would we need?

Patterns

Expectations are that children:
- Identify and make patterns
- recognise the characteristics of patterning
- become aware of group addition

Resources: Open space, tambour, drum/rhythm sticks
Concepts: Pattern recognition, sequencing, grouping, ordering

(a)

1 *Teacher talk: In a small jungle far away live the Patt and Ern tribes. The Patt tribe lives on the north side and the Ern tribe on the south.*
At night they meet to look for food.
This is what they do.
(Decide where north and south should be. Divide the class into the Patt and Ern tribes.)

2 *Teacher talk: The tribes wake to the sound of a drum. (Beat a one-two or one-two-three pattern.)*
What's the drum saying, can you whisper the pattern?

The tribes whisper the number pattern as they move to their meeting place.

Activities (a), (b) and (c) have a follow-through theme and can be taught in sequence or alone.

Resources: Classroom/ outdoors, coloured paper/card, textas, colours, art/craft materials
Concepts: Sorting, ordering, pattern-making and recognition, counting, group addition, more/less, number, sequence

Resources: Classroom, scraps/art/craft materials
Concepts: Problem-solving, halves, pattern identification.

3 When the tribes meet they find a partner and welcome each other by clapping the beat with them. Beat the drum until partners are formed.
4 Partners practise making different pattern beats using other body parts.
5 Children sit in a circle with partners. One by one, each pair plays their beat, other tribe members listen, say the number of the beat, and copy it.

(b)

1 *Teacher talk: The Patt and Ern tribes eat plants from the jungle.*
They eat only the food with patterns on it.
Do we have patterns on our plants?
2 Walk outdoors and observe the natural environment. Draw attention to the characteristics of patterning. Children find patterns on plants and trees.
3 Indoors children report on observations. Discuss the kind of jungle the Patt and Ern tribes live in. Suggest it might be filled with unusual fruits, vegetables and flowers. Using a variety of media and art materials children make patterned food which grows in the jungle.
4 In the class group, children show what they made, comment on and identify patterns.
Teacher talk: Tell me about your pattern.
Why is it a pattern?
Where does your pattern begin?
Where does the next sequence begin?
Can another tribe member continue your pattern?
Cover part of your pattern—can your partner tell you what is hidden?
5 Have children decorate the room with their 'plants'. Circulate, discuss and make comparisons between the patterns on different plants.
Teacher talk: What is the number of your pattern?
Can you add your pattern to someone else's?
How many things/groups in your pattern?
How many more/less than your partners?

(c)

1 Children become the Patt and Ern tribes.
Teacher talk: It's time to look for food in the jungle.
What will you carry your food in?

Children offer suggestions.
(Baskets from paper shapes could be made—this can be a problem-solving activity with children using only given materials.)
2 Children begin to look for food with a partner.
Remind them that the tribes only pick patterned food.

3 When the tribes return they have a special ceremony, as follows:
  (i) The tribes sit in a circle.
 (ii) The leader (teacher) asks members to call out the number pattern of a food item (for example three-two-three-two).
(iii) The leader then plays the number pattern on the tambour.
(iv) The tribes repeat the pattern by stamping their feet.
4 After the ceremony the tribes share the food.
Beat a pattern on the tambour after the ceremony to guide the tribes home. Tribes whisper the number as they walk home. When they arrive they quietly sleep.

Mathematics: Section B	Exploring space
	Expectations are that children:
	• recognise the perimeter of an area
	• understand basic spatial terms
	• develop an awareness of area and space

Resources: Open space, wool/string

Concepts: Curved/straight lines, length, longest/shortest, comparison, estimation, groups

1 Organise children into groups of three.
   Teacher talk: *You are three animal friends.*
   What kind of animals would you like to be?
   Two live together in the forest and the other one lives in the city.

2 Divide the working space into areas—representing the city and the forest. Children act out:
   Teacher talk: *The two forest animal friends want to visit their friend in the city.*
   Pack your suitcase; what will you take with you?

   Tell children that one of them is ready first and decides to begin the journey and leaves a trail for the other to follow. The first animal chooses from suitable materials to make a trail, for example wool, string, rulers. When the trail is completed the other forest friend follows it.
   The three friends are re-united in the city.

3 All the animals meet to discuss and compare the characteristics and length of trails and decide which was the shortest route to the city.
   Teacher talk: *Were the trails all the same length?*
   Which was the longest/shortest?
   Can you estimate how much longer/shorter?
   Which was curved/straight?
   Would the straight trail be longer/shorter than the curved one?
   How could you find out?

   Children find ways of measuring the trail.

4 The animal friends return to the forest via another trail taking their city friend with them.

Resources: Classroom furniture

Concepts: Estimation of size/length/width tessellation, comparison, longer/shorter, bigger/smaller, spatial terms

1 *Teacher talk:* *Pretend that our furniture is invisible.*
   I can't see my desk but I can feel it, so I know it's still there.

   In pairs children touch each piece of classroom furniture pretending that they can't see it, and describe its characteristics to each other.
   Teacher talk: *Can you trace around its shape?*
   Does it have straight/curved edges?

Are there any flat surfaces? How many?
Is the perimeter straight or curved?
How many corners does it have?

2 **Teacher talk:** *If the furniture stays invisible all day we'll probably bump into it.*
Let's mark out where it is.

Children select arbitrary units to place around the surface perimeter of the furniture.
With the perimeter defined the furniture becomes 'visible'.
Teacher talk: *Can you see the shape of the furniture now?*
Look at the perimeter. How wide/long is the desk?

3 Walk around observing and questioning children about their work.
Teacher talk: *Can you estimate how many red rods you used to go around the desk?*
How can you check?
What is the length of the perimeter?
Can you find a quicker way of counting?
Which side is longer/shorter?
Which has the larger/smaller surface?
How can you find out?
Can you find shapes to fill up the space inside the perimeter?
Estimate how many will fill up the space?

Resources: Open space
Concepts: Size, length, width, addition, area, perimeter, cardinal number, estimation, shape

1 **Teacher talk:** *The Wiggle family want a new house built.*
Let's make a floor plan for it.
How many bedrooms for a family of five Wiggles?
How many other rooms?
What size should they be?

Organise children into small groups of workers.
Allocate each the task of building one room in a given floor space.
Groups choose arbitrary units to outline the floor plan of the room.

2 In role as the boss observe workers in groups and where appropriate ask focus questions.
Teacher talk: *How many sides will your room have?*
Will all the sides be the same length?
How many sides are of equal length?
Can you estimate how long this side is?
What shape will it be when it's finished?
How many straws did you use on this side?
If your shape is a square will each side have the same number of straws?

3 When floor plans are completed groups record their work on paper to send to the Wiggle Family.

4 Compare the recorded floor plans with floor outlines. Discuss shape, number, length and materials used. Make size comparisons.
Teacher talk: Can you estimate how many popsticks were used for each room?
If you used unifix cubes for the kitchen instead of popsticks would you use more or less?
Which room is the smallest/biggest?
How can you tell?
How much bigger than the bathroom is the kitchen?
How can you work it out?
5 Groups complete reports to the Wiggle family by recording their responses on the floor plan sheet.

Resources: Open space
Concepts: Interval counting, pattern-making, group addition, sets, subtractions; estimation, spatial terms (around, between), problem-solving

1 *Teacher talk: You are a sculptor. A rich buyer wants some statues to arrange in patterns around his garden. Can you help?*

Children work with a partner with one assuming the role of sculptor and the other the lump of clay.
The sculptor moulds the clay into a statue.
2 When completed the statues are displayed in a row.
In role as the buyer inspect the statues.
Teacher talk: I like the statues.
Are there enough to make patterns of twos around my garden?

Pull one of the 'statues' out of the line. Have the sculptors put another one next to it.
Teacher talk: My garden is about this big (show the size of the space on the floor).
How many will I need to go around the garden in sets of two?

Children estimate.
Ask the sculptors to check estimates by placing the statues around the perimeter of the space indicated.
4 *Teacher talk: Were there enough statues?*
Are there any left?
How many statues made altogether?
Count the statues in twos.
Which is quicker, counting in ones or twos?
How many sets of two in the pattern?
Where does the pattern begin/end?
How much space between each set of two?
5 Repeat the activity with children swapping roles of sculptor and clay and/or using other number patterns. Children could also become other people and make different objects, for example horticulturists planning a garden setting.

Symmetry

Expectations are that children:
- recognise the characteristics of symmetry
- identify symmetrical objects
- are able to produce symmetry

○ **Resources:** Classroom, furniture, equipment, paper, pencils
Concepts: Half, middle, part of a whole, shapes, symmetrical, matching

1 In pairs, one child becomes a mirror into which the other performs actions.
Music could guide children's actions.
Partners swap roles and repeat.
2 *Teacher talk: Was the mirror image the same as the one performed?*
Both images were the same weren't they!
Are there things around us where one part is the same as the other?

Discuss shapes of things.

○ **Resources:** Classroom, furniture and classroom equipment, writing paper, pencils
Concepts: Parts of a whole, symmetrical, shapes, matching

1 *Teacher talk: Pretend you are scientists.*
Your job is to find symmetrical things—things with two parts that match.
Are you ready, scientists?
What will you need to take with you?
Right, let's go!
2 Circulate in role of chief scientist. Point out symmetry examples if necessary.
Teacher talk: What do you notice about these windows?
Can you find half of the window?
Does one part match the other?
Can you find other things with two matching parts which join in the middle?

Scientists record their findings.
3 The scientists report to government ministers. A small group of children in role as ministers question them about their findings.
4 Continue the activity with scientists exploring the natural environment for more evidence of symmetry.

○ **Resources:** Open space
Concepts: Symmetrical, line of symmetry

(a)
1 *Teacher talk: Did you know that human beings are symmetrical?*
How are we symmetrical?

Children sit opposite a partner and identify symmetry in each other.

2 **Teacher talk:** *Let's become symmetrical monsters! Join with a partner to become a symmetrical monster. Partners practise walking as monsters then present themselves in tableaux to the class. The audience identify the line of symmetry for the creatures and describe the symmetrical characteristics.*

Resources: Classroom, building blocks
Concepts: Symmetrical construction

Activities (a) and (b) have a follow-through theme and can be taught in sequence or alone.

(b)

1 **Teacher talk:** *Symmetrical monsters live in Symmetry Land. What do you think their homes might look like? What do the streets look like? What will other things in Symmetry Land look like?*
2 In small groups children build Symmetry Land out of blocks.
3 Circulate commenting on and observing children's work.

Solids

Expectations are that children:
- identify characteristics of solid shapes
- understand that solids are 3-dimensional figures
- become aware that solid shapes have flat or curved surfaces

Resources: Building blocks, solid shapes
Concepts: Enclosed space, height, same, inside, outside, surface, 3-dimensional

1 **Teacher talk:** *A long time ago some people built tall towers to show how rich they were. Each person wanted their tower to be different from anyone else's. But there were some things the same in all the towers. Do you know what they were?*

Children make suggestions.

2 **Teacher talk:** *Pretend we are rich people building towers. With a partner children use building blocks to build towers. If some children finish early they may add extensions.*
3 When towers are completed children walk around in role of rich people commenting on other people's towers.
   Teacher talk: *Look at this one. It's pretty tall. Is it the tallest? What's different/the same about all of them?*

Focus on criteria relating to solids.
   Teacher talk: *Can you describe the shape? Is it like a plane shape? Why not? Is there a roof on the tower? Does it have walls? What name can we give the outside walls? (surface) Is it a solid shape?*
4 Children return to the class group and select a solid shape from an assortment provided which best matches their structure, and make comparisons between the two.

Resources: Classroom, empty grocery packets, containers, etc., scrap materials, masking tape, scissors, glue

Concepts: Edges, corners, top, bottom, vertices, surfaces (curved/flat), sorting, grouping, size, ordering

(a)

1 *Teacher talk: Who's been to the supermarket lately? The shelves are always full of groceries, aren't they? Who puts them there?*

Discuss.

2 *Teacher talk: Let's pretend it's our job to stock the shelves. We need a supermarket first though!*

Children turn the classroom into a supermarket using desks and chairs.
Provide a wide assortment of empty grocery packets and containers.
Tell children to examine them closely to make sure they are not damaged.
Model the inspection of a few items, pointing to relevant characteristics, for example 'The edges/surfaces/corners of the carton seem all right!'

Teacher talk: I'd better go over it carefully just in case.
Number one edge is OK.
Number two edge is OK.
Number three edge is OK, etc.
All of the twelve edges of this box are in good condition.

Children work with a partner and inspect the cartons in the same manner.
These could be marked off on a recording sheet.

Activities (a) and (b) have a follow-through theme and can be taught in sequence or alone.

3 Have children sort the grocery items on the shelves (for example washing powders, fruit juices, etc.).

4 Assume the role of a fussy supermarket inspector and guide children around the supermarket checking that groceries are grouped according to their category.

Teacher talk: Is the margarine in the right place? How do you know? Should the shampoo be near the soap? Why? And so on.

Children can also arrange cartons in order of size.

Resources: Classroom, empty grocery packets, containers, etc.
Concepts: Solids, surfaces, sides, edges, vertices

(b)

1 *Teacher talk: The supermarket is set up. There's only one thing left to do. Let's go shopping!*

Tell children that there is a 'special' on today.

They get one free grocery item if they accurately describe the characteristics of a container (for example curved surface, two edges, etc.) to the check-out operator. Put a limit on the number of items each child can buy.

2 Select four children to be check-out operators. They decide the amount of each grocery item.

3 Children make shopping bags before beginning.
As children finish the bags they go shopping. At the check-out, the operator decides whether the description of a container warrants a free grocery item.

Mathematics: Section C

Night and day

Expectations are that children:
- compare night and day
- develop a basic understanding of how night and day occurs

Resources: Open space
Concepts: Day, night, sunrise/sunset, summer, warmth

Activities (a), (b) and (c) have a follow-through theme and can be taught in sequence or alone.

Resources: Open space
Concepts: Daylight, night, heat radiation, revolution, rotation

(a)

1 **Teacher talk:** *Close your eyes, imagine it's a summer day.*
You're at the beach.
Look at all the lovely cool water.
Let's go for a swim!

Children improvise.
2 Tell children they are tired out from swimming and will rest on the beach.
Teacher talk: *Close your eyes.*
Listen to the seagulls/waves as you fall asleep.
(Make the 'sh, sh, sh' sound of waves to create atmosphere.)
3 **Teacher talk:** *You've been asleep a long time now.*
You're feeling cold—wake up slowly.
It's all dark—where's the sun gone?
Where is it? Which way did it go? And so on.

Assess children's understanding of darkness according to their responses. Ascertain whether children know the direction the sun may be seen rising/setting?

(b)

1 **Teacher talk:** *Where does our daylight come from?*
Does anything happen to the sun at night?
Does anything happen to the Earth?
Let's see if we can find out.

Choose a small group to form a circle in the centre of the space and become the sun. Have them facing and stretching their arms outward to show heat radiating. Another two children join hands facing each other and become the Earth.
2 How does the sun's light reach the Earth?
Does the Earth/sun move? Where does it go?

Discuss, then have the Earth and sun demonstrate suggestions.
3 Children representing the Earth move around the sun. Invite the audience to comment on accuracy of movement. Have other children become the Earth and demonstrate their understanding of the Earth's movement.
4 Guide children to conclusions by stopping the Earth's movement now and again to ask focusing questions.

Teacher talk: *Which side of the Earth has the most light now?*
How much light on the surface facing away from the sun?
Which surface is warmer? Why?

(c)

Resources: Open space, toy spider/bug, masking tape
Concepts: Morning/afternoon, temperature

1 **Teacher talk:** *It's early morning—you are a tiny bug. Come out from behind your leaf to enjoy the morning sunshine. It's lunch-time—find something to nibble on. Goodness the sun's hot! Find a shady place to rest.*

Children improvise.

2 Discuss the variations in temperature during the day. As in the previous activity children personify the sun and the Earth.

3 Stop the Earth's movement periodically. Children take turns to put a toy bug on the Earth where morning is occurring.
Teacher talk: *Noon is usually the warmest time of day. Show where it would be on the earth.*

A child places the toy bug where noon would be occurring. (Leave the bug on the 'Earth' as it moves around the sun.)

4 Continue the activity, repeating the above steps with different times of day.

Measuring time

Expectations are that children:
- identify things that measure time
- understand the importance of measuring time

Resources: Classroom, outdoor environment
Concepts: Summer, autumn, seasons, passing of time, shadows, temperature

1 **Teacher talk:** *Once upon a time people didn't have clocks. Did people need to know the time then?*

Discuss and reflect on activities we do which were also done a long time ago (for example sleeping, eating, celebrating, etc.). Ask how people would know when it was time to do those things.

2 Walk outdoors during late morning or early afternoon. Have children pretend they are rural workers before modern technology.
Organise children into groups.
Teacher talk: *It's summer-time.*
It's time to collect the fruit from the plants you planted.

Children improvise. Circulate making comments and asking focusing questions.

Teacher talk: What do you have growing this year?
How long will it take you to pick all your fruit?
Where will you put it?

3 In the class group, discuss the amount of time the workers
   will work in one day.
   Teacher talk: How will they know if it's time for a rest?
   Will they know if it's lunch-time or time to go home? How?
   Children become workers again and try to discover answers
   through the improvisation.

4 The class discuss their experiences and reflect on visible signs
   which indicate the time of day (sun, shadows, temperature).

Resources: Open space,
large sheet of paper,
textas, situation cards (see
below)
Concepts: Measuring
time,
timetables/schedules,
o'clock, passing of time

1 *Teacher talk: Do we need to know the time? Why?*

Record responses on a large sheet of paper.
Teacher talk: What could happen if you didn't know the
time?
Let's find out!

2 Organise children into groups. Each group selects a situation
   card for discussion, for example:
   (a) It's a school day. You are fast asleep. The alarm clock
       doesn't go off.
   (b) You are playing with friends. You want to stop when it's
       time for your favourite TV program. No one has a watch.
   (c) You're going shopping. The car breaks down. You decide
       to catch a bus. You don't have a watch. How will you
       know what time the bus arrives?
   (d) You are having a party. Everyone is arriving at two o'clock.
       What might happen if you don't know what the time is?

3 Children improvise the situations. They make conclusions
   about what may occur as a result of not knowing the time,
   for example being late, missing appointments, missing out on
   things.

Resources: Open space,
twelve hoops, pencils,
paper plates, cardboard
strips, split pins, textas,
scissors
Concepts: Estimation,
measure of time (hour,
day, week), number,
sequence, ordering (after),
night/day, clocks, o'clock

1 Assume the role of the town mayor. Tell children you need
   some clockmakers for a special job.
   Teacher talk: We need a new clock for our Town Hall.
   The Queen is coming to a reception next week and the clock
   doesn't keep time properly!
   You must work night and day to get it finished in time.
   Do you think you can get the job done quickly?

2 Choose a small group of clockmakers to make the plan of the
   clock face.
   Teacher talk: How long will the plan take to complete?
   What's the time now? (Draw attention to the classroom
   clock.)
   Can you estimate what time it will be when it is finished?

3 The Mayor begins the plan of the clock by placing two children inside a hoop to represent the number 12.
Teacher talk: *What hour comes after 12 o'clock? What hour comes after that?*

Clockmakers continue the plan by adding children to represent other numbers until the clock circle is complete.

4 The remaining children become the hands of the clock. Children move around as the clock's hands. Stop the clock at intervals and ask children what time it is.

5 The class records the plan by making decorative clocks with paper plates. Display the clocks. In role as townspeople children vote for the design they like best.

Resources: Open space, books on the history of time, sand, small clear plastic bottles, masking tape, string, small heavy object, glue scissors, sheet of paper, textas
Concepts: Clocks, measuring time, time-measuring devices

1 **Teacher talk:** *Could you measure time without a clock? Would you know when it's time to stop doing something? Would you know how long it takes to do things?*

Make a list of indoor/outdoor tasks children would like to time.

2 Organise children into small groups of inventors to discuss how activities could be timed without clocks.

3 In a class circle, groups share ideas. Provide groups with books and illustrations of time devices used through history.

4 Inventors sit in a circle and discuss their ideas. Place an assortment of scrap materials in the centre. Inventors explore materials and make instruments to measure time, for example:
—sand, small clear plastic bottles—join to make sand clocks
—string, weight (plasticine, sinker)—pendulum
—cardboard, rulers/straight sticks—shadow clocks
—plastic squeeze bottle, water—water clock

5 The inventors test clocks by timing activities listed, for
example:
   It takes 15 drips to bounce a ball 10 times.
   It takes 10 swings of the pendulum to bounce a ball 10
   times.
Discuss whether a uniform measure of time is important.

Money in our lives
Expectations are that children:
- understand the purpose of money
- become aware of the value of money
- develop a basic understanding of money use in our
  community

Resources: Open space,
pictures of people in work
occupations
Concepts: Value of
goods/services, much,
enough, purchase/
expenditure

1 **Teacher talk:** *How do you spend your money?*
Let's go shopping and see!

Organise children into groups. Each group improvises
shopping at a particular place. Circulate and ask focusing
questions.
Teacher talk: *What are you buying today?*
How much money do you have to spend?
Will that be enough money for. . .?

2 Children sit in a class circle and say what they bought.
Teacher talk: *Did everyone buy something?*
Can you actually spend money but not buy a 'thing' with it?

3 Children think of times money is spent but no tangible
purchases made.
Teacher talk: *What do you get from the doctor/hairdresser?*
Do you buy 'things' from them?

Show pictures of people in various occupations and ask
children what they get from them. Introduce the terms
'goods' and 'services'.
Cut pictures from magazines; write captions using these
labels.

Resources: Open space,
large sheet of paper,
textas
Concepts: Wages/salaries,
goods/services,
expenditure

1 List occupations of children's parents.
Teacher talk: *Do your parents get paid for what they do?*
How do you know?
Who gives them money?
Let's see if we can find out!

2 In pairs children improvise an occupation from the list.
Children close their eyes and reflect on their chosen role.
Teacher talk: What will you be doing?
What will you need in your job?
Will other people be working with you?
Where will your job take place?

Children discuss, then improvise.
3 Circulate and ask focusing questions. Particularly comment on handling of money and how payment occurs for the job done.
4 Choose some children to present their improvisation to the class.
The class identifies how money is being used and how payment occurs. Children also define whether goods/services are involved.

Resources: Open space, small pieces of card, pencils, textas, scissors
Concepts: Grouping, sorting, money—recognition, recording, value; cost, expensive, more/least

1 *Teacher talk: What is your favourite toy?*
Where does it come from?
How much do you think it costs?

Each child writes a price tag for their toy.
2 A small group become shop assistants. Others become toys in a shop. Shop assistants sort toys into categories and write price tags for each.
3 Shop assistants sit in a row facing the toys and compare/coment on the prices of different toys.
Teacher talk: Would a doll be the same price as a small ball?
What might be the more/least expensive toy?

Discuss values of different toys.

Resources: Open space, large sheet of paper, textas, coins
Concepts: Money recognition, spending, amounts

(a)
1 *Teacher talk: Who's got spending money today?*
Where did you get it from?
What are you going to do with it?
What will happen to it when you spend it?

Discuss.
2 *Teacher talk: Money seems to travel quite a bit doesn't it!*
I wonder what stories it would tell if it talked!

Children choose partners. Give every pair a coin. One child assumes the role of the picture/symbol on the coin. The other interviews the coin about its travels.
3 Some children show their interviews to the class group.
List places where the coin travelled, for example:
—the bus
—the supermarket
—the picture theatre
—the bank

Activities (a) and (b) have a follow-through theme and can be taught in sequence or alone.

Resources: Open space, coins

Concepts: Money recognition, money—value, estimation, addition; sorting/grouping

(b)

1 Each child examines and mimes the character/symbol on a coin. Help children work out the role they will act out.
Teacher talk: Is it a person/animal/other?
Can it move? How? What does it do?

Children practise becoming the character.

2 Individuals present their mime to the class. The audience says what coin they think is being represented.

3 In role as the coin character children find their personal space. Call out the value of a coin; 'coins' of the same value group together. Others estimate the value of the group. Add the 'coins' to confirm the estimate. Do this several times with different value coins.

Mathematics across the curriculum

Language

Make a picture timetable of school activities; write captions—is there a pattern of events?

Write labels for pictures of workers; estimate how many words will fit on cards of different sizes.

Write stories about:
    Four-headed, four-legged monsters
    Number Country
    A circus
    What I want to be when I grow up!

Write a recipe for vegetable soup—what kind of measures will be used?

Write a sign advertising a circus—which words will be biggest/smallest?

Design/write a time-tabled program for a circus performance.

Make a Big Book showing how maths is used at home/in the community.

List mathematical things done today.

Write poems inside symmetrical shapes of their topic, for example a butterfly poem inside a butterfly shape.

Mathematics

Make budgets for spending pocket money.

Estimate weight of equipment in the room—can you check accuracy?

Draw a plan of the school building; give each room a number to indicate size from smallest to largest.

Estimate the length of a basketball court—check your accuracy quickly.
Find ways to measure round shapes.
Draw a patterned t-shirt for yourself.
Build structures of different sizes; measure the dimensions.
Fill empty packets to demonstrate weight shown on the box.

Society

Find patterns in clothing; record them.
View tribal/village life at a museum—note patterns on utensils/accessories.
Invite people to talk on maths used in their jobs.
Make a shopping list; estimate money needed; visit a shop, check prices.
Set up a supermarket/clothes shop with used cartons/old clothes—price each item.
Group pets according to certain criteria, for example long hair/size, etc.
List ways people keep warm—compare temperatures in different schoolrooms.
Look at pictures of buildings around the world; record shapes/sizes.
Estimate/compare distances from children's homes to school.
Estimate height of school buildings.

Science

Make a weather chart; are there noticeable patterns?
Examine indoor plants for leaf patterns; record.
Have a friend outline your shadow in chalk at different times during the day—measure the shadows.
Make pancakes; estimate the cooked size by the quantity of mixture used.
Have a 'science circus'—what can be performed with light and shadows?
Stand a bottle in hot water; place a balloon over the opening—what changes occur to the balloon? Measure the widest part of the balloon.

Environment

Walk outdoors, record animal tracks—where do they begin/end? Measure the length.
Collect natural materials, make two or three different patterns.
Count the shade trees in the yard—how many should be planted to make a row of uninterrupted shade?
Plant seeds/plants—what size plot is needed? How much space between plants?

Observe movement of animals—estimate the speed/distance they travel.
Estimate/compare the time to walk a winding/straight path through a park.
Observe shapes in nature; record them on coloured paper; cut out, suspend.
Draw/cut out an outdoor scene into fractions, paste back together; leave out a part. Guess what is missing.

Art
Use straws, clay or macaroni to make a necklace pattern.
Paint pictures of people's homes; display in size order around the room.
Draw/paint clothing suitable for unusually shaped creatures.
Paint a sign to fit in a given space.
Cut pictures from magazines into fractions; make an abstract poster.

Music
Compose body/environmental pattern beats to accompany favourite songs.
Conduct an improvised orchestration of sound patterns.
Clap out a rhythm; others repeat and add a new rhythm. Keep building on.
Use percussion instruments to make sound patterns; identify the numbers.

Health
Share a healthy lunch; find patterns in fruit/vegetable slices.
Draw natural foods; estimate the cost of each item; compare with fast foods.
Bring fruit from home; estimate and compare weight.
Which of our senses help with estimation of weight/size?
What medicine do you take when you are ill? Draw the container/bottle; write appropriate dosage on the label.
Make 'fraction' soup using a variety of vegetables.
Personal space—how much do you need to feel comfortable? Discuss/measure.

Technology
Find out about early communication.
Make up sound patterns to send messages with.
Design/make hats for outdoor jobs; draw apt picture-patterned headbands.
Draw a plan of a bedroom you would like; make model furniture.

Make boxes to hold unusual things, for example a five-wheeled machine.

Make a model of a circus tent, using a given number of materials.

Make an enclosure for a small animal.

Make a house frame with straws of unequal length.

Make a set of plans showing the school buildings viewed from different angles.

References

Aboriginal Studies R-3
Education Department of South Australia, Government Printer, South Australia 1987

Air—Starting Points
Su Swallow, Franklin Watts Australia, NSW

Art Works Book 1
Kathryn Puddey & Susan Mackay, Longman Cheshire, Australia 1990

Drama and Learning R-7
Drama Across the Curriculum
Windows on Practice Publication, Education Department of South Aust., 1991

Drama Anytime
Jill Charters & Anne Gately, Primary English Teaching Association, Rozelle, NSW 1986

Drama is Primary
Publications & Information Branch, Education Department of Victoria, Melbourne 1982

Encyclopaedia of Nature & Science
Bay Books, Sydney 1974

Energy
Ron Thomas & Jan Hipgrave, Macmillan Company of Australia, 1991

Energy Sources
Brian Mackness, Golden Press Pty Ltd, NSW 1984

Environment
Education Department of South Australia, A.B. Caudell, Government Printer, SA 1992

Everyday Science
The Question & Answer Encyclopaedia Series
Michael Gabb, Sackett Publicare Ltd, London 1978

Exciting Ideas for Frazzled Teachers
Christine Syme, Dominie Publication, Holmes McDougall, Australia 1983

Exploring Together
A Primary Science Program
Cheryl Jakab, Horwitz Grahame Books Pty Ltd, NSW 1988

Health Education
Years R-3 Teachers Handbook
Education Department of South Australia, D.J. Woolman, Government Printer, SA 1983

How Big is the Moon?
Whole Maths in Action
Dave Baker, Cheryl Semple, Tony Stead, Oxford University Press, Australia 1990

How to Teach Primary Drama
Bruce Burton, Longman Cheshire, Australia 1991

Language is Fun
Teachers' Book—Level One, Book One
Brian Cutting & Helen Depree, Sunshine Books, Rigby Education, Australia

Learning and Living
Social Studies Curriculum Guidelines R-3 Units
Education Department of South Australia, D.J. Woolman, Government Printer, SA 1982

Look! Book 3
  Australian Science & Technology

Cyril Gilbert & Peter Matthew,
Longman Cheshire, Australia 1990

Loving and Beyond
  Science Teaching for the
  Humanistic Classroom

Joe Abruscato & Jack Hassard,
Goodyear Publishing Co. Inc.,
Santa Monica, California 1976

Mathematics for the Very Young
  A Teachers' Resource Book

Judy Tertini,
Horwitz Grahame Books Pty Ltd, Sydney 1986

Maths in Context
  A Thematic Approach

Deidre Edwards,
Eleanor Curtain Publishing,
South Yarra, Vic., Australia 1990

One Approach to Integrating Drama
  into the Primary Curriculum

Primary Interest Group,
Victorian Association for Drama in
Education, 1992

Open-ended Tasks in Maths
  R-7 Mathematics

Windows on Practice Publication,
Education Department of South Aust., 1991

Our Land
  Landcare Activities for Upper
  Primary Landcare for Kids Series

Catherine Buxton,
National Soil Conservation Program,
Department of Conservation,
Forests and Lands, Victoria, 1989

Puddles and Wings and Grapevine
  Swings

Imogene Forte & Marjorie Frank,
Incentive Publications Inc.,
Nashville, Tennessee 1982

Science Fun
  Discovering the World Around You

The Australian Make & Do Series,
Incentive Publications Inc,
Nashville, Tennessee 1985

Soil Magic
  Landcare Activities for Middle
  Primary Landcare for Kids Series

Catherine Buxton,
National Soil Conservation Program,
Forests and Lands, Victoria, 1989

The How and Why Wonder Book of
  Weather

David Houghton,
Transworld Publishers, London 1977

What Happens If. . .?
  (Science experiments you can do
  by yourself)

Rose Wyler,
Scholastic Book Services, USA 1974

Why We Have Day and Night

Peter F. Neumeyer & Edward Gorey,
Young Scott Books, New York, USA 1970